"We need adventure. Mankind has always needed adventure, and perhaps we need it more than ever in the technological civilization of the twentieth century."

—Chay Blyth

"A thrilling tale of achievement. Blyth emerges as something unique, someone a lot larger than the majority."

—*Scotsman*

"Buoyant and humorous."

—*Daily Telegraph*

THE IMPOSSIBLE VOYAGE

Chay Blyth

BALLANTINE BOOKS • NEW YORK

SBN 345-03382-5-150

This edition published by arrangement with
G. P. Putnam's Sons

First Printing: July, 1973

Printed in the United States of America

Cover art by Chris Foss

BALLANTINE BOOKS, INC.
201 E. 50th Street, New York, N. Y. 10022

To Maureen

Contents

Illustrations in Colour and Monochrome

(between pages 112 and 113)

Author's Acknowledgements

In presenting this book to the public I feel that I must express in particular thanks to the British Steel Corporation, without whom the whole voyage could scarcely have taken place. Within the corporation my gratitude goes out especially to Mr Cartwright for his constant backing and encouragement, to Mr Will Camp, for his imaginative foresight, and to Mr John Dunkley and Mr Phil Wolfinden, for their tireless administration. High on the 'thanks' list too comes Mr Terry Bond for his initiative in first suggesting an approach to the British Steel Corporation, and for his constant guidance and friendship. Then I must thank Mr Robert Clark, for his genius in designing *British Steel*, and the men at Philip's Yard, Dartmouth, who built her. I must also acknowledge a particular debt to the Royal Southern Yacht Club and its members, notably the Commodore Mr Bill Cottell, Mr Frank Allen, and Mr Chris Waddington, and (of course) their wives. I must also thank Lord Watkinson, Patrick McNair-Wilson, MP, Eric Moody, David Russell, Eric Downey, Neville Wood, Brian Cooke, Michael Hearn, Dr H. L. Proctor, Ken Watkins, Eric Lee, Charlie Brooker, David Dyer, Rupert Dove-Meadows, George Chandler, Betty Ridley, C. A. Rich, Roger Norman, Dennis Casbolt and Ben Bradley. Help and encouragement came too from Cliff Pearson and other members of the *Sunday Mirror* staff.

Many firms gave food, gear and equipment for the voyage. My debt to them is very real and they include Blacks of

Greenock; Derek Howell of BCB Ltd, Cardiff; Brooke Bond Oxo Ltd; Schermuly Ltd, of Dorking; Bowater Scott Corporation Ltd; Lewmar Ltd, and Sparlight Ltd, of Emsworth; Ratsey and Lapthorn Ltd, Cowes; Brookes and Gatehouse Ltd, Lymington; Henri-Lloyd Ltd; Nestlé Co Ltd; H. R Spencer, of Cowes; C.A.V. Lucas; International Paint Co Ltd; British Melamine Tableware Co Ltd; Bovril Group Marketing Ltd; W. A. Baxter and Son Ltd; Dunlop Ltd; H. J. Heinz and Co Ltd; Batchelors Foods; Honda (UK) Ltd; Lyle and Scott Ltd; Rolex; Guinness Ltd; Schweppes (Home) Ltd; Thames Marine Ltd.

I must acknowledge my debt to Mr J. R. L. Anderson who edited my logs and who wrote the prologue to my book. But most of all my heartful gratitude goes to my family, Maureen, Samantha and Maureen's mother, Mrs Kathleen Morris. No one, not even I, can ever know the sacrifice they have made.

Prologue

The Aim and the Achievement

by J. R. L. Anderson

The Aim and the Achievement

Demonstrably, the title of this book is invalid: what was once called 'impossible' cannot be so regarded any more. Yet it retains a certain, rather attractive, validity, in the sense of that saying current in the Army which Chay Blyth served with such distinction 'The impossible we do at once; miracles take a little longer.' It was in that spirit that Chay tackled the impossible; it is in that spirit that he made it possible.

It is necessary here to consider precisely what Chay's voyage was. It has been presented as various sorts of achievement – a non-stop circumnavigation of the globe the 'wrong way' round, an 'uphill' voyage round the world, for instance. These are telling phrases, carrying an element of truth, but they don't really mean much. The world has been circumnavigated from east to west many times in history; it was the passage of the early circumnavigators, Magellan and Drake, it was the passage, over seventy years ago, of the father of singlehanded ocean sailing, Joshua Slocum, in a homemade wooden boat. True, much of it can be called 'uphill' in the sense that it is against the prevailing wind systems, particularly in rounding the Horn but in any ocean passage over many months there are bound to be long periods of windward sailing.

Chay's navigational achievement was not in the direction

he took, but in his route, keeping to high latitudes at th
southern tip of the globe. He has explained in his own na
rative what this means, but I must stress it again here. Sout
of roughly 40° S, in the so-called 'Roaring Forties' there
little land on the earth's surface until you get to the co
tinental mass of the Antarctic. A band of sea encircles th
globe, and in this band there is nothing to break the force
either wind or swell. From the primeval start of our spinnin
world's endless journey in space the wind has blown u
checked over these lonely seas; the 'fall out', as it were, of a
the storms that have ever raged remains to create the mo
formidable swell to be met anywhere on the earth's surfac
When this swell is broken into waves by a new storm th
height and power of the sea are beyond description.

The clipper ships of the great days of sail, bringing te
from China or wool from Australia, made their passag
home eastwards round the Horn, to take advantage of th
prevailing Westerlies in these high latitudes. It was a form
idable passage, even for those great and well-manned ship
Chichester, Rose and Knox-Johnston have made it alone i
little wooden sailing boats – magnificent human achiev
ments, not in any sense belittled by Chay's voyage.

But Chay's voyage was yet more formidable in that h
chose deliberately to sail into the teeth of those powerf
Westerlies that helped to blow the others home. This wa
not so much a matter of being on the wind for long perio
at a stretch – as I have said, any small-boat sailor making a
ocean passage can expect the discomfort and strain to boa
gear and human nerves and frame of considerable perio
on the wind. Chay's problem was that the very structure
the globe was against him; everything determined by te
restrial physics, wind systems, swell, wave-formation, move
generally *against* his path. To sail round the world his wa
he had, in the inelegant but vivid phrase, to buck th
system.

No one has even attempted his voyage before. Other mariners circumnavigating the world from east to west have gone north after rounding the Horn, to the warmer and kindlier seas of the mid-Pacific. And they have taken time, refreshing body and spirit in the delectable archipelagos of the South Seas. Chay allowed himself no respite, and he sailed against time as he sailed against wind and sea, driving himself and his boat day and night for close upon ten months.

Chay completed his voyage, Hamble to Hamble, in 292 days. (Had it not been for Cowes Week and the need for making careful arrangements for Chay's welcome, he could have knocked three days off his passage. He was off the Eddystone on August 2, and deliberately slowed up to time his arrival at Hamble for August 6. He could certainly have achieved a passage time of 289 days, but as things were 292 it had to be.) For comparison, Robin Knox-Johnston, in *Suhaili*, sailing non-stop round the world the other way, made his voyage from Falmouth to Falmouth in 313 days. For further comparison, those other singlehanders, Sir Francis Chichester in *Gipsy Moth IV* took 274 days from Plymouth to Plymouth, with forty-eight days spent in Australia, and Sir Alec Rose in *Lively Lady* took 354 days from Portsmouth to Portsmouth, with thirty-six days in Australia and New Zealand. These comparisons do not mean much, for in no case is like being compared with like. Chay and Robin Knox-Johnston both sailed singlehanded and non-stop, but one sailed east to west, the other west to east, and Chay's 59-foot *British Steel* was not far short of twice the length of Knox-Johnston's 32-foot *Suhaili*. Chichester and Rose both took time off in Australia for rest, repairs and replenishment of stores, but Chichester's 53-foot racing machine *Gipsy Moth IV* was as different from Rose's elderly 36-foot *Lively Lady* as *British Steel* from *Suhaili*. At the time of their various circumnavigations Chichester was sixty-five, Rose fifty-nine, Knox-Johnston twenty-nine and Chay thirty.

Unlike as their achievements are, however, some points of comparative interest can be made. For those who think in terms of records and league tables, Chay can fairly claim the record for a non-stop singlehanded voyage round the world, his time of 292 days from port to port having handsomely beaten that of his only challenger, Robin Knox-Johnston. But *Suhaili* was not a fast boat, and Knox-Johnston was not greatly concerned with making a fast passage. For sheer speed Chichester remains in a class by himself, though as he did not sail non-stop and he was able to make repairs and undertake considerable refitting in Australia, his passage times on his homeward voyage cannot properly be compared with those of vessels that have not touched port. Nevertheless, his ocean racing performance in *Gipsy Moth IV* was outstanding, and his record for a singlehanded voyage round the world remains unbroken. And he sailed at more than twice the age of Chay and Knox-Johnston.

But arguments over records may be left to statisticians. The times can be made more (or less) meaningful at will by devising ocean racing handicaps for the various boats. This makes good bar-talk; it is little more. Each of these men, in his different way, set out to fulfil himself; each succeeded. Each possesses in a high degree a human quality – or rather, complex of qualities – that I have called elsewhere 'the Ulysses factor'*, an urge or need to see for himself what lies over the hill, across the desert or beyond the sea. Had they lived earlier in history they would have sailed through the Pillars of Hercules to discover Britain, crossed the Atlantic to discover America, found the source of the Nile or been the first to set human foot on the North Pole. These things having been achieved, they invented their own challenges, to

* *The Ulysses Factor*, by J. R. L. Anderson. Hodder and Stoughton, 1970.

sail round the world alone, to sail round the world alone and
without putting in at any port, to sail round the world alone
in high southern latitudes from east to west. That great
mountaineer, the late Lionel Terray, called his book on
climbing *Conquistadores of the Useless*. Useless? In the
sense that there is no market for real estate on the summit of
Everest, that no new pelagic fisheries are likely to be developed as a result of Chay's voyage, all these achievements
of high human endeavour are useless. In the sense that
Chay, Chichester and their peers have opened new horizons
for mankind they may be held to be among the true inspirers
of this century; men who have used their own wits and limbs
to show that there is a challenge in man himself to climb the
unclimbable, to do the impossible, to which the individual
can still triumphantly respond.

Chay Blyth had good parents and a happy home, but few
material advantages in his upbringing. Apprenticed to a
knitwear manufacturer in his home town of Hawick he decided that factory life was not for him, and at the age of
eighteen joined the Army. His choice of the Army, and,
within the Army, of the Parachute Regiment, gave him the
opportunity of hard, physical endeavour that his young
mind and body needed – mind as well as body, mind even
more than body, for the qualities of discipline and self-
discipline, trust in comrades and self-reliance that are required in a good soldier are mental things. He became the
youngest sergeant in his regiment, and qualified in a wide
range of skills, from parachute jumping to survival in the
Arctic. Then, as a purely personal expedition, he rowed
across the Atlantic in an open dory with John Ridgway, an
officer in his regiment. He was getting things in focus for his
personal fulfilment, progressing from the corporate adventures of Army life to Atlantic adventure with one companion. Next he set off to test himself alone, to sail round the
world single-handed in a small family cruiser. That adventure

ended in South Africa, when he decided it would be folly to go on – a decision that required a disciplined, hard courage, different from, but not less real than, the courage of setting out. On his way home from South Africa he began thinking of what to try next. He was tempted by two projects: a canoe trip on the headwaters of the Amazon, and a singlehanded circumnavigation of the world from east to west.

His approach to both was practical. Any such expedition would need money, and he had little money. He had done a few unusual things in his thirty years, but his position as a married man with one child was no different from that of millions of other men dependent on their wages. He had a job as a sales representative, his wife worked as a telephonist; their joint earnings were enough to provide a comfortable small home, certainly no more. A garden, a car, perhaps a sailing dinghy, as the years advance maybe membership of a golf club – that is the limit of physical horizon for most men in Chay's position. Most of us, even if we start with wider personal horizons, are compelled – or feel compelled – to limit them. Chay accepted no such compulsion. That is his importance for the rest of us.

He studied in public libraries the literature of the Amazon and books on wind systems and ocean currents of the world. He calculated his own chances of success or failure, reckoned coolly what each of his proposed adventures would cost, and considered how to set about paying for them. He had no money, but he had ideas. And in certain circumstances ideas can be turned into money.

In earlier periods of history a man with an idea looked for a personal patron – monarch or pope, rich nobleman or wealthy merchant. There is nothing new in sponsorship. The first circumnavigators of Africa were sponsored by an Egyptian queen, Columbus was sponsored by Queen Isabella of Spain, Cabot by Henry VII of England. There are fewer monarchs now, and those that remain have so many calls on

their private purses that young men with visions are not
likely to touch them. Nor do modern monarchs engage in
personal financial enterprises as their ancestors did.

There are still rich men, but in Western society, at any
rate, great wealth is seldom any longer really personal; it is
held in trust, hedged with devices to meet taxation, and
seldom accessible to finance an adventurous private whim.
Taxes have reduced personal wealth generally to a point
where there are few individuals left to bestow patronage.
The arts, which have always depended on patronage, now
have State sponsorship channelled to them through the Arts
Council.

But as the older sources of patronage have dried up, industry has – at least to some extent – replaced them. Modern
industry is Protean, and a board of directors is as capable of
commissioning an artist to decorate its boardroom as were
medieval popes and bishops to encourage artists by employ-
ing them to decorate cathedrals. The money that once
flowed to the Church now flows to commerce, and at least a
minority of company directors (as it may have been a minority of medieval ecclesiastics) accepts that man does not
live by bread alone. Chay might once have financed his
voyage by persuading a temporal prince or prince of the
Church to help him to the discovery of a Great Southern
Continent, with a return to be looked for in gold to exploit
or souls to convert, or both. The return that he could offer to
twentieth-century industry was publicity. He considered his
two projects carefully – the Amazon and the South Pacific –
from the point of view of which would be more likely to
attract commercial sponsorship. He decided on the voyage.
Then, by what seems a near-miracle of luck, he enlisted the
help of a brilliantly imaginative young public relations man,
working not in the lush metropolitan pastures of PR, but in
the Midlands. Chay wanted a steel boat for his voyage, for
the strength it would give him in standing up to the battering

that he knew he must receive. Terry Bond believed that if anyone was to provide such a boat for such a voyage it should be the nationalized British Steel industry. Between them they put up a case that convinced the steelmen. Chay got his boat, and the backing that made his impossible voyage possible.

Now it is necessary to keep a very clear head about these commercial aspects of Chay's voyage. Had his father been a duke instead of a railwayman, and had Chay sold an inherited estate to finance his voyage, no one would feel that his adventure was in any way demeaned by commerce. Having no estate to sell, he sold an idea. And nearly as much courage was shown by the men who bought his idea as he himself showed in carrying it out.

A modern board of directors, particularly if they direct a nationalized industry, is subject to checks and inhibitions that did not worry medieval princes, either of commerce or the Church. If Columbus had lost his life instead of getting back to Spain with news of his dramatic discoveries in the West, nobody would have blamed Queen Isabella. If she had lost money on him, people would have reckoned that it was hers to lose; in any case, it was little enough money in relation to the revenues of the Spanish Crown. One mad seaman more or less – what did it matter? No one outside his family would have bothered much had Columbus come to grief.

Had Chay met disaster, the British Steel Corporation would have been subject to damning questions in Parliament. How dare a nationalized industry use public money to encourage young lunatics to their deaths? Even without disaster there might be damning questions: how could the Corporation justify the expenditure of public money on a harebrained scheme to sail singlehanded round the world? What good did it do? How could wage demands in national-

ized industries be resisted if money was wasted on this sort
of thing?

The British Steel Corporation took the risk. This book
shows how triumphantly Chay justified it. As a British citi-
zen, and (I suppose) a part-owner of the nationalized steel
industry, I can only congratulate the BSC on this particular
bit of risk-taking. Man does not live by bread (or even by
steel) alone. Chay's voyage in *British Steel* may be useless,
but it has done more to enable us to hold up our heads in the
world than most recent acts of national policy. National
prestige is an odd thing, defying rational analysis. A football team winning the World Cup probably does as much
for its country as most Prime Ministers. British economy
may be laggard, our domestic politics may be in a mess – *but*
a thirty-year-old Scotsman (and the rest of the United King-
dom may bask in his reflection) is the only man in the world
to have sailed singlehanded, non-stop around the world
from east to west.

The question of sponsorship of such adventures needs to be
considered more deeply. Splendid as is Chay's achievement
– and the sponsorship which made it possible – obviously
industry cannot survive by financing young men (or even
young women) to sail about the world in small boats. As a
result of Chay's success, one may expect that the British
Steel Corporation (the Coal Board, British Railways and the
Gas Council as well, no doubt) will be deluged for years
with requests from adventurous people for sponsorship.
Most such requests will be doomed to disappointment –
and, alas, I must add, rightly so doomed. The board of any
great industry or commercial firm has vast responsibilities,
and in spite of what newspapers write from time to time
when an industry gets into a mess, most members of such
boards have a high sense of personal responsibility. They

are spending other people's money, many thousands – or hundreds of thousands – of other people may be affected by their actions. In relation to the profit and loss account of the British Steel Corporation, expenditure on Chay Blyth was a bagatelle; but the cost of a postage stamp is miniscule in relation to the expenditure of even a small business, yet a good businessman does not neglect to keep an eye on the postage bill. Chay's appeal to the BSC was of value because it came at a particular time, and in a particular set of human circumstances. The British steel industry was relatively newly nationalized, there had been much anti-nationalization propaganda, and there was point in a dramatic demonstration that national ownership did not mean the dead hand of bureaucracy over everything. Moreover there was a particular case for giving exceptional publicity to the use of steel in British yacht-building. Yacht yards in Holland have been building small boats in steel successfully for many years. Relatively few British yards are equipped to build in steel. The yacht industry is small in comparison with the motor industry, but it is by no means negligible. It is obviously in the steel industry's interest that British yards should be encouraged to build in steel. Expenditure on Chay's adventure could, therefore, be justified on three counts – as a demonstration of a newly nationalized industry's readiness to support individual initiative, as advertising the strength and general qualities of British steel when subjected to exceptionally severe conditions, and as giving particular publicity to the virtues of steel in British yachtbuilding. That Chay's request for sponsorship came at a time when all these considerations had weight was partly a matter of luck, partly a matter of good judgement by his advisers. More important than all this, however, was Chay Blyth himself. It is one thing to have an idea, even to be prepared to undertake a formidable task; to fire other men's imaginations with the peculiar *rightness*, the *necessity*, of such a task is something quite other. Chay has this quality, which is compact of courage, skill, integrity and determination, but also beyond all of them.

Even so, his was not a request to be granted lightly. Chay had first to satisfy shrewd men that he was not a lunatic, that he knew what he was doing and had a reasonable chance of carrying out his plans. More important, he had also to satisfy the BSC that his risks were calculated, that he was not likely to be foolhardy, and that if things went badly wrong he would have the courage to give up. His record helped in all this, but his own personality helped even more – as one of the men who originally interviewed him put it, 'He answered no question quickly; he thought hard and seriously before he said anything at all.'

For its part, the BSC did everything it could for Chay's psychological as well as physical protection during his voyage. All steel for the construction of his boat was inspected by the Corporation's own experts – that was an obvious step. Less obvious was the care that was taken in drawing up an agreement with Chay. The BSC paid for the building of his boat, and it was therefore legally the Corporation's property. The intention was for ownership to be transferred to Chay if he carried out his side of the bargain; but how was this to be defined? At first it was agreed that ownership should pass to Chay as soon as he had crossed a particular line of longitude. That seemed reasonable enough; but the Corporation had second thoughts. Suppose conditions were very bad: might not an exhausted Chay be tempted to drive himself beyond the limits of safety in order to cross the line and acquire ownership of the boat? To meet this possibility the agreement was varied to provide that Chay should be given the boat when the Corporation was satisfied that he had used his best endeavours to earn it, without specifying any geographical line or limit to be reached. This seems to me a remarkable example of humane farsightedness.

With the most humanely drawn contract, however, sponsorship of this sort has its dangers. The tragedies of Donald Crowhurst, David Johnstone and John Hoare remain in many minds. Commercial sponsorship was in no way responsible for any of these personal disasters – yet without the existence of sponsorship it may be felt that none of them would have happened. It was not a newspaper contract that sent Johnstone and Hoare to their deaths in an unsuccessful attempt to row the Atlantic, but without a newspaper contract perhaps they would not have set off when they did. Crowhurst was not sponsored by the *Sunday Times* but that newspaper's offer of £5,000 to the first man to sail single-handed and non-stop round the world certainly encouraged his unhappy venture, and he left ill-prepared in order to meet the starting date to be eligible for the prize. To what extent the offer of prize money for anything may be held to imply responsibility is arguable: are the promoters of a boxing match, entered freely by the contestants, responsible if one man suffers an accidental brain injury, and dies? Much human progress has come from the offer of prize money for feats of difficulty and daring – the *Daily Mail's* prize encouraged Blériot to fly the Channel in 1909, and had an important influence on the development of the aeroplane. If all goes well, nobody asks awkward questions; if there is a disaster, the questions may be very awkward indeed. I do not much believe in vicarious or consequential responsibility. A man is ultimately responsible for his own actions, and if he meets disaster in attempting something that he wants to do, I doubt if others can be fairly blamed. But one cannot be dogmatic about this; there is room for many different points of view, and certainly there are circumstances in which the promoter of a dangerous enterprise could be held to have acted not merely irresponsibly, but wickedly. The British Steel Corporation had to think of all this. They took a brave, imaginative decision in backing

Chay, and the outcome was a triumphant success. But the decision would have been just as brave, and just as right, had things gone wrong.

Chay got his backing from the BSC, but anyone who thinks that this made the preparations for his voyage easy is mistaken. The BSC paid for his boat, but all the planning and preparing remained his. The account of how he and his wife Maureen tackled the immense task of collecting equipment and stores for the voyage, and supervising the fitting out of *British Steel* while, for much of the time, both had to stay at work to earn their living, and for all of the time had to look after their young daughter, is in some ways the most moving part of his narrative. Chay's boat was built for him, but for the rest he had to rely on his own resources. First the garage, then the bedroom of his bungalow became a warehouse for stores. Maureen shopped for up to eighteen months' supply of food, and varnished every tin herself (imperative for storing tins of foodstuffs on small boats, but a back-breaking and horrible job to do). In January 1970, Chay's boat was still a dream. In August 1970 she was launched, and in August 1971 she brought him home after sailing 30,000 miles. Such a performance has scarcely been matched in maritime history. It is unlikely to be surpassed, and it is an integral part of Chay's real achievement.

A boat derives from the brain and hands of man, but every boat that has ever sailed has a personality of her own. This may reflect the personality of her builders and crew, but it is a reflection too subtle for analysis, bringing out points of character unguessed in their human originals. Anyone who saw *British Steel* sail into the Hamble river on August 6th, 1971, could be pardoned for thinking that she had just crossed the Channel instead of having sailed round the world. Her condition was an astonishing tribute to her designer and builders, and to the good sea-husbandry of her lone skipper and crew. She is an enormous boat for one man to handle; Chay's mastery of her through the storms and crises of 30,000 miles of ocean was made evident by her safe return. But no one saw Chay and his boat when they met their gales alone. We did see them as they made their way up the Solent, surrounded by a huge spectacular fleet. Chay's nonchalance in handling a 59-foot boat under sail when the smallest error would have brought a collision demonstrated a bond between man and vessel that can be felt, but not described. *British Steel* was conceived in Chay's mind. She was given life by Robert Clark, her designer, and by the men who built her in Philip's yard at Dartmouth. At his press conference after he landed Chay was more eager to praise his boat and designer than to claim credit for himself. The praise was merited, but it reflected, too, a generosity in the man that had also become part of the personality of his boat. If you are sensitive to such things, the moment you climb on board *British Steel* you feel that here is a good and *generous* boat, a boat that will give everything she has to her master, that in any circumstances will do her best to help. The partnership of Chay and *British Steel* was a wonderful one. It was fitting that they should be greeted by the Prince of Wales, the Duke of Edinburgh, Princess Anne and the Prime Minister (Mr Edward Heath) and tens of thousands of their fellow-countrymen.

So Chay's voyage ended, a triumph for a man (and the woman who stood by him), for a great British industry, for a British yacht designer and the workmen of a British boat yard. A momentary triumph, or a lasting one? The Solent has seen the homecoming of many triumphant British ships and seamen, the men of war which for centuries have sailed from Portsmouth, the great liners and merchantmen sailing from Southampton. Can the successful outcome of one man's whim be even remotely comparable with the achievements of navies and the ships that earn Britain's daily bread? Chay's voyage was undoubtedly a victory of some sort; but of what sort, a victory over what? Why should royal personages and humbler folk in their thousands flock to the Hamble to cheer him? What did they cheer?

The cynic may say, 'Given such high-powered publicity, people are bound to come. Crowds will flock to anything – and forget what they have seen next day.' The cynic here is wrong. Publicity alone can perhaps make a pop-star. It cannot make a hero. And Chichester, Rose, Knox-Johnston, Chay Blyth and a handful of other modern adventurers *are* heroes, national heroes in the true sense. They have not driven enemy fleets from Britain's shores, they have not brought news of undiscovered continents. But they have, each of them, discovered a new world, and other people sense this. They have manifested that quality in man which makes for the survival of the individual in a world ever more subject to mass tensions, mass unbeliefs, and massed living. Chay and his peers have found new worlds for themselves; the rest of us can scarcely hope to penetrate *their* worlds, but it is enough to know that they exist. We may become resigned to our own place on the conveyor belt of twentieth-century living (or what passes for living), but we respond with slightly quickened pulses to those who show us that this is *not* the only way of living. We may have neither the skill nor the wish to round Cape Horn by ourselves, but *because* Chay sailed alone against the westerly gales at the rim of the world we can derive new meaning from a dinghy, a canoe, or hill-walk. Chay and his peers are the openers of doors in our own prisons. That is their real achievement, and that is why we salute them.

Commercial sponsorship is not essential to this sort of achievement, but it widens greatly the range of possibilities. Chay, I think, would have found some way of sailing the world singlehanded, or of exploring the Amazon, whether

or not he obtained commercial help: his rowing of the At
lantic with John Ridgway was a wholly private enterprise
The British Steel Corporation provided him with a bette
boat than he could have hoped to acquire on his own, an
enabled him to accomplish in a year and a half what migh
have taken him a decade on his own. But he had served hi
apprenticeship; the BSC's decision to back him wa
thoroughly justified. This does not mean that any youn
man with a distaste for factory work can look to industry fo
financial backing for an adventure, or has any cause to fee
aggrieved if such backing is denied him. Chay's achievemen
is proof that a man can do what he wants without help from
public school or university friends, or any other fortuitou
social aids. But Chay's achievement is the outcome of year
of hard self-discipline and dedicated self-training. It is
splendid thing that the nationalized steel industry shoul
have helped Chay to fulfil himself; but such help mus
remain rare. It would falsify everything Chay stands for i
his achievement led others to think, 'Look what can be go
from sailing round the world!' Chay's achievement is not i
what he got, but what he gave.

J. R. L. Anderson

Chay Blyth's Narrative

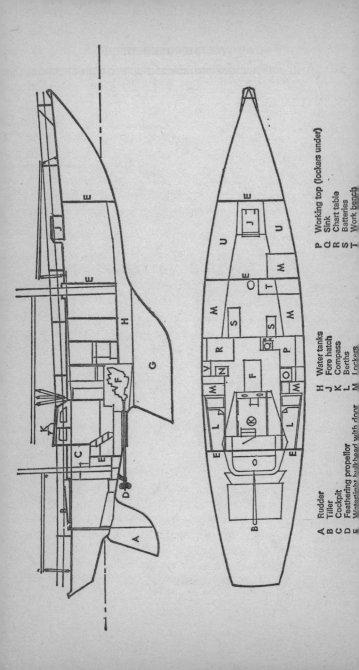

A Rudder
B Tiller
C Cockpit
D Feathering propeller
E Watertight bulkhead with door

H Water tanks
J Fore hatch
K Compass
L Berths
M Lockers

P Working top (lockers under)
Q Sink
R Chart table
S Batteries
T Work bench

CHAPTER ONE

A Dream of Adventure

Begin at the beginning and go until you come to the end –
that is Lewis Carroll's advice to anyone with a tale to tell. It
is excellent advice. But how do you identify a beginning?
On October 18th, 1970, I sailed from the Hamble in the
ketch *British Steel* to attempt a voyage never sailed before,
an east–west circumnavigation of the globe, singlehanded
and non-stop. That was certainly a start. But a beginning?
Heavens, no: it was the climax to months, indeed years, of
thinking, planning, and preparation.

But one must begin somewhere. Did this adventure really
begin on that April day in 1966 when I walked into the office
of Captain John Ridgway, of the Parachute Regiment,
at Aldershot and volunteered to accompany him on his
project of rowing the Atlantic in an open dory? Or did
it begin on Christmas Eve 1962 when I married Maureen
(of whom there will be much in this book)? Or in 1958
when I joined the Parachute Regiment when I was eighteen?
Or on May 14th, 1940 when I was born? You could make a
case for any of these beginnings. For practical purposes,
though, I'll start on a day in November 1968, when Maureen
and I were sailing home together from South Africa in *Dytiscus*, a 30-foot family cruiser of the Kingfisher class in
which I'd tried, and failed, to sail round the world. *Dytiscus*
was a splendid little boat: she'd carried me non-stop for over

9,000 miles, but she was not designed for the great gales and tremendous seas of the Roaring Forties on the lonely edge of the world. In appalling weather south of the Cape of Good Hope (the Cape of Storms was its earlier name) I'd decided that it would be madness to go on, and put back to Port Elizabeth. There, Maureen had flown out from England to join me for the voyage home. *Dytiscus* was game enough, but when running before a strong wind and a following sea she was rather a handful and it was all I could do to hold her. I was complaining about this one day when Maureen said, 'Well, why not sail round the world the other way?' It was a chance remark, she was laughing me out of a bad temper. I had other things to think of then, but her words stayed in my mind. Why not?

We were aching to get home to our daughter Samantha, then aged fourteen months, but the weather was against us. We left *Dytiscus* in the Azores and went on to England by air (I returned to collect *Dytiscus* later). Before I could think of any more adventuring I had first to get a job, and I was lucky to be offered one that I could do from our home at Portsmouth, as a sales representative for Schweppes. I liked the job, travelling round pubs and yacht clubs representing the Schweppes company, and I think I did it fairly well, for before I left I came fourth in the order of business done by Schweppes representatives. But I found it hard to settle down. I'd had nine years in the Parachute Regiment, becoming sergeant at the age of twenty-one and serving in the Middle East, Cyprus, Europe, Scandinavia, Malta, Canada and Aden. I'd completed an Arctic Survival course and a Desert Survival course, taken part in the world's longest canoe race, and made over a hundred parachute descents. I'd been seconded as an instructor at the Eskdale Outward Bound School. In 1966 I'd rowed across the Atlantic with John Ridgway, from Cape Cod to Kilronan, in the Aran Islands in the dory *English Rose III* – ninety-two days in an open boat. That attracted a good deal of publicity and I was in demand for giving lectures all over Britain. Towards the end of 1967 I left the Army and bought a partnership in a garage. There was a clash of personalities, this venture into business was not a success. In 1968 I wanted to enter for the Singlehanded Transatlantic Race and Westfield Engineering, the builders of *Dytiscus*, generously lent her to me for the purpose. Even more generously, they agreed to let me have her when I changed my mind and decided to have a go at sailing round the world instead, making a race of it with Robin Knox-Johnston, John Ridgway and the others who sailed in what was later taken up by the *Sunday Times* as the Singlehanded Round-the-World Race. That was the voyage that ended in South Africa. I had never formally entered for the race, so although I disqualified myself by putting into South Africa I could scarcely be said to have lost, but I felt very much that I had failed. Maureen's quick response to my need in flying out to South Africa to sail home with me – though she had never sailed before – was a wonderful restorative, but I still felt that somehow I had let her down and everybody else by not going on to complete my voyage round the world singlehanded.

In South Africa I had met an old friend from the Parachute Regiment, a fellow Scot, Chick Gough. He had left the Army to play football for Charlton Athletic and subsequently emigrated to South Africa to become a leading footballer there. He was a godsend to me in that bleak period obsessed by my sense of failure, and we discussed a great project of crossing the Andes and then travelling the whole length of the Amazon by canoe. This is something that I have always wanted to do, and Chick's enthusiasm did me a lot of good. I kept thinking of the Amazon when I got back to England – but I kept thinking of Maureen's remark about sailing singlehanded the 'wrong way' round the world, as well.

The 'wrong way'? The first voyages to circumnavigate the globe were made from east to west, out from Western Europe through the South Atlantic, round the tip of South America into the Pacific, and home via the East Indies and the Cape of Good Hope. The first man to plan a successful voyage round the world was the Portuguese navigator Fernao (Ferdinand) Magellan: he did not live to complete it, but one of his ships did. Magellan sailed in 1520, convinced that there must somewhere be a way through the unknown (in fact, non-existent) continent, Terra Australis Incognita, which geographers then thought extended from South America to the South Pole. The Atlantic coast of South America was known, and so was the Pacific coast, though it was not then called the Pacific – Magellan gave that great ocean its name; before him it was called simply the Southern Sea. Magellan had no reason to disbelieve the geographers who held that a great southern continent was needed to 'balance' the land-mass of Europe and Asia in the north, but he felt sure that there must be a strait or passage through it to link the oceans on either side. With immense fortitude he survived disaster after disaster to discover, and to force his way through, the strait that still bears his name – the Magellan Strait. This runs between the tip of continental South America and the islands of Tierra del Fuego, although Magellan did not know that they were islands; he thought that Tierra del Fuego was part of the great Southern Continent. In 1576 Drake repeated Magellan's voyage in his *Golden Hind*. He worked his way through the Magellan Strait but on entering the Pacific he was blown back south-east by a formidable gale. Whether or not Drake ever saw Cape Horn is doubtful, but he was blown back far enough to discover open water south of Tierra del Fuego and to leave his name on the map – the wide stretch of sea between Cape Horn and the South Shetland Isles of the Antarctic is still called Drake Passage or Drake Strait. Drake's discovery of open water south of

South America was of vital political importance at the time, and was kept (as far as possible) a secret. The Spanish and Portuguese claimed a monopoly of trade in South America and the South Seas: if Magellan's strait was the only passage from the Atlantic to the Pacific, it could be fortified and ships of other nations kept out; if, however, it was possible to sail round South America without using Magellan's strait, the monopoly could not be preserved. In spite of efforts to keep Drake's discovery a secret, news of it gradually leaked out among seamen, and in 1616 a Dutch merchant called Le Maire equipped an expedition led by Wilhelm Cornelius Schouten, an able sea-captain who had worked for the Dutch East India Company, to try to find a route from the Atlantic to the Pacific other than by the Strait of Magellan. Schouten sailed on south of Cape Virgins at the entrance to the Magellan Strait and discovered a passage between Tierra del Fuego and Staten Island which he called after his patron Le Maire Strait. He went on to round the great cliff which he identified correctly as the last land of the archipelago at the tip of South America and he named it Cape Hoorn, after the little town in the Netherlands which was the home town of his patron and of many of his crew. Cape Horn it remains today.

So all the earliest navigations were east to west, and yet we consider it the 'wrong way'. It is truly a formidable passage. This is because the spin of the world makes the prevailing winds at its southern tip blow from the west. Look at the globe, and you will see that apart from the tip of South America, Tasmania and the South Island of New Zealand there is next to no land anywhere south of Latitude 40 deg S. The Westerlies sweep endlessly around the world, building up a swell which has surged for millennia, with scarcely anything to break it save the great basalt cliffs around Cape Horn. Magellan, Drake and Schouten all had tremendous difficulty in beating their way westwards, and navigators

who followed them sometimes gave up in despair. A ship
might try for a month to round Cape Horn, or to force a
passage through the Magellan Strait, only to be blown back
again and again. After the opening of the Pacific by Captain
Cook in the eighteenth century, and the settlement of Australia and New Zealand, the clipper ships serving the Far
East went out via the Cape of Good Hope and home via the
Horn, a circumnavigation west-to-east which takes advantage of the prevailing Westerlies. Before the opening of the
Panama Canal, virtually the only ships attempting a westward passage of Cape Horn were those from the eastern
seaboard of the United States making for San Francisco
and the west coast, and often they had a dreadful time of it.
After the opening of the Panama Canal, hardly any vessel,
sail or steam, has needed to attempt a westward passage.
Almost all small boat circumnavigations have been from
west-to-east – that was the way of Chichester, Rose, and
Knox-Johnston, the way I set out to try to sail round the
world in *Dytiscus* in 1968.

The westward passage has been made by small-boat
sailors, of course. Joshua Slocum, the founding father, as it
were, of singlehanded cruising, took his *Spray* through Magellan and round the world from east to west in 1895–8. But
Slocum took three years over his voyage, putting into port
whenever he felt like it on the way. Dr David Lewis made a
westerly circumnavigation in his catamaran *Rehu Moana*
between 1964 and 1968, a wonderful voyage, with his two
very young daughters on board. He also went through Magellan, and he, too, spent some years over the voyage, taking
time off for various purposes at several intermediate
stops.

What haunted me was the possibility of attempting a
westerly circumnavigation singlehanded and non-stop.
Moreover, instead of going north after rounding Cape Horn
and making for home through the kindlier seas of the South

Sea islands and the East Indies, I wanted to stay in the empty ocean of the far south, not leaving those lonely high southern latitudes until I turned north for home on rounding the Cape of Good Hope. That would be a voyage to excite any man – and no one had ever attempted it before.

I did not – could not – make up my mind at once. In those early months of 1969, after I had come home from my voyage in *Dytiscus*, I was still much attracted by the idea of an Amazon adventure. Almost as soon as I got back I put the problem to my friends Frank and Audrey Allen, who had invited Maureen and me to stay with them for a few days while we 'settled down'. Frank asked me what I was going to do. I said, 'Well, I've got to look for a job first, and goodness knows what that's going to be. After nine years in the Parachute Regiment about the only thing you're really qualified for is the job of being a "hired gun", and there are not many vacancies for that.' Then I said, 'Frank, I'd like your advice.'

'Only too pleased,' he replied.

'Well,' I went on, 'Maureen and I have been thinking, and I'd *really* like to do one of two things – to cross the Andes – and canoe down the Amazon, or to sail westwards round the world against the prevailing winds and currents.'

Frank laughed. 'You're not exactly settled yet,' he said. He looked at Maureen, and she smiled and shrugged her shoulders.

'Now I know you are both crazy,' he continued, and he gave me a little lecture about the need to be satisfied with the adventure we'd just had. But Frank is a good friend and a truly understanding man. After his little lecture, he went on, 'If you really must go on adventuring, then I think the westwards sailing trip is by far the greater project. To go against the Roaring Forties – that would be something.'

Adventure, however, has to be paid for. To contemplate either project seriously I should need to find a sponsor: who would be interested in putting up the money to sponsor me? I discussed this with Frank, and we both felt that a westerly circumnavigation would be the venture more likely to attract support. On leaving Frank and Audrey we paid a visit to Newcastle-on-Tyne, where Maureen's mother lives, and I spent a lot of time in Newcastle Public Library studying books about the Amazon and the wind systems of the world. When we got home to our bungalow at Portsmouth I set about getting a job, and duly got my job with Schweppes. But I couldn't forget my projects. I telephoned a Fleet Street reporter and went to London to ask his advice. He thought it doubtful if I could get much financial help for either venture, but considered, on the whole, that the Amazon project was probably the better bet. That was not particularly encouraging. It looked as if I'd better try to settle down to routine as best I could.

In March I went up to the Birmingham Boat Show, and there I met a man called Terry Bond. He had been on the staff of the *Birmingham Post* but was setting up in business on his own as a consultant in Public Relations. I walked round the Boat Show with him and found myself liking him very much. He asked if there was any other really great sea adventure left. I said that the only thing I could think of was a circumnavigation westwards, and added that no one was likely to rush into that because it would need a very special boat and only the best in equipment, which would make it very expensive. Terry asked, quite casually, 'If you got the boat you wanted, would you do it?' I said, simply, 'Yes.' I did not explain then that I had lived with the idea for months and had already gone into it in great detail.

How does an ordinary chap with no family fortune behind him set about sailing round the world singlehanded? My father was a railwayman working at Hawick, in Scotland, and I was born at Hawick in 1940. I went to Hawick High

School but I left school at fifteen to be apprenticed as a frame worker in a knitwear factory. I wanted more from life than working in a factory, so when I was eighteen I did what many young men with a sense of adventure in them have always done – I joined the Army. I joined what I shall always think of as the best unit in the Army, the Parachute Regiment. That gave me a number of fine assets in life, among them a tough training in survival, some splendid friends and a sense of responsibility. But it certainly did not give me riches. The Atlantic row in 1966 rather unexpectedly brought me a certain amount of money, from the book which I wrote with John Ridgway, from TV programmes, lectures and the like. I'd used this to buy my share in the garage I'd mentioned earlier, and to acquire our bungalow at Portsmouth. My garage venture, as I've said, was not a success. I'd been able to make my round-the-world attempt in 1968 only because of other people's kindness – R. A. G. Nierop, of Westfield Engineering, who lent me *Dytiscus*, Neville Wood of the Windward Sailing School at Southsea, who gave me sailing lessons and helped me to study navigation, Frank Allen, Bill Cottell, and members of the Royal Southern Yacht Club, who helped in all sorts of ways, and a number of firms who gave me stores and equipment for the voyage. From my point of view that venture had also been a failure. Had I succeeded in sailing round the world non-stop I might have won the five-thousand-pound prize offered by the *Sunday Times* and profited in all the other ways by which the world rewards success. As things turned out I got no farther than South Africa and spent most of what little money I had left on Maureen's flight to South Africa in order to sail home with me. *Dytiscus* was still in the Azores: I had still to go out to the Azores to bring her home. I was responsible for Maureen and Samantha. In all these circumstances it seemed madness to contemplate a westerly voyage round the world which would cost, at the very lowest, some tens of thousands of pounds.

But I could not put the idea out of my head. If an idea is good enough, it can sometimes be translated into money. Maureen was on my side. She knew how important my dream was to me and instead of telling me not to be silly she comforted and encouraged me in every way possible. Yes, I wanted twenty – thirty – forty thousand pounds. But I had something to offer in return. If I could bring off a voyage that had never been attempted – let alone achieved – before, it would be worth money to the firm or firms that sponsored me. Modern commerce is a strange business. Companies find it worthwhile to sponsor golf tournaments, tennis matches, horse races, all sorts of human activities. Could I find a sponsor for my voyage? I thought, perhaps, I could.

I made endless calculations. I decided that the boat I needed should have a steel hull, to withstand the appalling strains it would have to meet. I thought at first that I'd like a schooner rig, partly to spread the area of sail over two masts (an advantage to a singlehander in limiting the area of individual sails), partly to ensure that if I lost one mast there'd be a reasonable chance of keeping the other. I studied wind and current charts, worked out distances and courses.

In the late summer of 1969 Schweppes gave me leave to go to the Azores to collect *Dytiscus*. Shortly before I left I decided to write to Terry Bond. Marking my letter 'Private and Confidential', I wrote:

Since I arrived back in the UK, and, indeed, sailing back from Africa, I have toyed with an idea. On arrival I started getting some information and details on the proposed trip, and I now find that it is definitely possible. The trip is basically to sail around the world non-stop – but the other way from the normal route, that is, from east to west and not west to east. On looking at it just like that you may not see the implications, but I can assure you that it is a very different kettle of fish from the other trips. It would take too long, and I doubt if I could give you the full picture in a letter, so will not attempt it. I would like you to handle the PR side of it. My own view is that it can be planned and directed well in advance. If you accept, I strongly suggest a meeting as quickly as possible. Because time is my greatest enemy I would like to see you within the week – I leave for the Azores very soon. There is a terrific amount to do, mainly from my side initially, but I cannot get started till I see you. If you and your company take it on, I must see you immediately, and suggest you drive to Portsmouth in an afternoon, stop overnight, drive back next morning. That way we get maximum work for minimum hours.

Terry responded at once. He came down to see us at Portsmouth and we had a long talk about everything. Terry thought that since my plans envisaged a steel boat we should first approach the steel industry for possible sponsorship. He was as enthusiastic as I was about the worthwhileness of the adventure. I left for the Azores much happier in my mind.

I had hoped to have two friends with me to sail back in *Dytiscus*, but when the time came neither could get away from his business, so I had to go alone. The trip back took only fourteen days, but I had to spend a week in the Azores sorting out a technical problem. The crane which had lifted out *Dytiscus* had been handed over to NATO, and according to the officials in the Azores it couldn't now be used for anything except NATO business. As it was the only crane that could do the job I was in a pickle. However, by chasing all over the place I finally obtained permission from someone in Lisbon for the crane to be used, and after that all went well.

Maureen came out in a motorboat to meet *Dytiscus* and she greeted me with the news that there was a letter from

Terry. He began encouragingly 'I have made some progress', and went on to say that he had discussed the project
with a friend of his, Patrick McNair-Wilson. He was a
Member of Parliament and he knew a lot about the steel
industry because he was a spokesman for the (then) Conservative Opposition on iron and steel. McNair-Wilson's
advice was that we should try to have a meeting with Mr W.
N. A. Camp, (then) Head of Information Services for the
British Steel Corporation. Terry asked me to telephone him
with some dates when I could be in London for such a meeting.

I had, of course, to get back to my job, and it wasn't all
that easy to find time for meetings in London. McNair-
Wilson had to attend the Conservative Party Conference,
and all sorts of other things had to be fitted in. It was nearly
the end of October before our meeting with Mr Camp could
be arranged. Meanwhile, Terry and I prepared a detailed
'presentation' of our project, with maps and a sketch of the
sort of boat I wanted.

Our meeting, when it came, seemed to go fairly well. Mr
Camp and his Steel Corporation colleagues listened to all I
had to say, and then asked a lot of questions which I
answered as well as I could. Of course they couldn't give us
a decision on the spot. Mr Camp said that there was much
that he would have to go into, and that he would write and
let us know whether the Corporation could sponsor our project or not.

Then came a nail-biting time. Waiting is always hard to
bear, and I am not good at waiting – I am better at action, or
at least trying to get things done. I thought of the words
which a well-wisher at Cape Cod had said to us as we embarked in *English Rose III* to row across an ocean – 'You
will need patience, above all patience.' I did my best to be
patient, but I'm afraid I rather badgered Terry, arguing that
we should have other irons in the fire and that we should be

approaching other possible sponsors in case the British Steel Corporation turned us down. Terry, however, was wise and firm: it would not be right, he said, to offer our project to anyone else before we had had a definite answer from the BSC.

At last the answer came. On December 6th Terry received a short letter from Mr Camp. It said:

> There has inevitably been quite a lot of discussion about your Chay Blyth proposal, but I am happy now to tell you that we are willing, in principle, to support the project.
>
> We would, however, want to have quite a big say in the design of the boat and other matters, and before giving a definite decision it would be necessary for the matter to be fully discussed between yourselves and Mr W. F. Cartwright, a member of the Board who will be taking a close interest in the project and who is a yachtsman of considerable experience.

I can't even begin to describe my feelings – what *do* you feel when a dream suddenly comes true? I had felt I had something to offer the British Steel Corporation, but I was asking a fearful lot. Asking, too, for a great deal to be taken on trust. There were times during the long wait when it all seemed impossible. Now – the whole thing suddenly became real.

Of course, we were not out of the wood. There was that meeting with Mr Cartwright ahead of us. Could I convince him? Yes – I thought I could.

Mr Camp's description of Mr Cartwright as 'a yachtsman of considerable experience' was a considerable understatement. He had been ocean racing since before the war, he was a member of the Royal Yacht Squadron, and undoubtedly one of the most distinguished of British yachtsmen. Before nationalization of the iron and steel industry he had been managing director of the Steel Company of Wales, and on nationalization he had become a deputy chairman of the British Steel Corporation. I didn't know it then, but he was the best friend my project could have had. During our long wait, when I thought nothing was happening, Mr Cartwright had been standing up for me against a good deal of opposition, particularly from one of the eminent experts whose opinion on my plans had been sought by the BSC. This man poured several buckets of cold water on my ideas. He called my scheme 'naive', and described me as 'a good jockey' rather than an experienced seaman. He thought my approach was that of a 'stunt man' and he saw no reason why my idea of a windward circumnavigation should capture anyone's imagination, though he conceded that a race of some sort might 'sustain interest'. However, he did give me credit for 'boundless courage and verve'.

This might have been the end of the matter but for Mr Cartwright. He replied to the expert objections with a memorandum that combined imagination with a wonderful understanding of what adventure really means. I knew nothing of all this when I went to see him but I have since read his memorandum, and realize how much I owe to his support. He conceded that 'there is no real point' in sailing round the world, but he would not accept that interest could be sustained only by some kind of 'race'. What stirred interest, he maintained, was the way in which something was done. He recalled Humphrey Barton's crossing of the Atlantic from Falmouth to New York in 1950 in his 25-foot *Vertue XXXV*. That had not been a race, Barton had not sailed singlehanded; he had set out simply to test his belief that a very small boat *could* cross an ocean against the prevailing winds, a thing that at that time had been considered very difficult to do. From that voyage everybody had learned a lot. Mr Cartwright also defended me against the charge of being 'a stunt man'.

'Blyth', he wrote, 'may not be an experienced seaman in one sense, but he has a number of considerable voyages to his credit.' Mr Cartwright wholly supported my idea that the boat for my proposed voyage should be built of steel. He did not like my suggestion of schooner rig – and in this he was certainly right. The ketch rig that I finally adopted retained the advantage of giving me a subsidiary mast for safety's sake, and was undoubtedly much better for performance to windward.

Most important of all, Mr Cartwright would not have my project dismissed out of hand. He agreed that some of my ideas were 'naive', but he thought that that could be put right. He understood instinctively what my motives were, and what I was trying to do, and he wanted to help if he could.

Terry and I met Mr Cartwright for the 'follow up' discussion suggested by Mr Camp on the last day of 1969. I could scarcely have been in worse shape for the meeting, for I was in the throes of a horrid bout of flu. I went to London overnight, with a cold so heavy that I could scarcely speak, and a temperature of over 100°F. Terry was shocked. We decided that the best treatment would be a very hot curry before going to bed. We tried it, and maybe it helped to keep me on my feet, but I was still pretty ill in the morning. However, I was not going to let *anything* interfere with the meeting, and Mr Cartwright must have made allowances, for we came away not only with an agreement that the BSC would sponsor the voyage, but with the practical suggestion that Mr Robert Clark should be invited to design the boat, and that she should be called *British Steel*.

The BSC's headquarters are in Grosvenor Place. Mr Clark's office was not far away, in Albemarle Street. I was so overjoyed that I forgot I was feeling ill, and we went round to see him at once. What this distinguished yacht designer must have thought of us, I just don't know. He was patient and polite, but it was an extraordinary situation. Here were two young men out of the blue, one admitting to next to no knowledge of boats, the other with such a heavy cold that he was hard to understand. They wanted a yacht that would cost thousands of pounds, she must be built in steel, she must be built straightaway, and the man with the cold said that he proposed to sail her singlehanded from east to west around the world. More bewildering still, this strange pair announced that the British Steel Corporation would be willing to pay for the boat.

Whatever his private thoughts Mr Clark listened to what we had to say, agreed that he could design the sort of boat we wanted, and quoted a fee in pounds, which he quickly amended to guineas on the ground that guineas were so much easier to work with! As soon as we'd gone he took the precaution of telephoning the British Steel Corporation – to learn that our statements, however wild they may have seemed, were in fact quite true. So began another fine working partnership, a really decisive step in making my dream come true. That evening I went down with pleurisy.

CHAPTER TWO

From Dream to Reality

Maureen and I had planned to go to a New Year's Eve Ball at the Royal Southern Yacht Club, but when I got home from London she made me go straight to the doctor. He told me to go to bed at once, saying that I'd developed pleurisy. I was too excited to feel worried. My chief trouble was that I wanted to tell Maureen about everything that had happened in London, but the pleurisy made it so difficult to breathe that I could scarcely speak! However, with some long gaps while I struggled for breath I did manage to describe most of what had happened at our meetings with the British Steel people and with Robert Clark, and although it was an odd way to see in the New Year, for me it was quite a pleasant evening. Maureen, I'm afraid, was considerably worried, for I looked grey and ghastly, and was really pretty ill.

Next morning – New Year's Day 1970 – Maureen moved a bed into the living-room, so that I could see and hear whatever was going on. Robert Clark telephoned, but she said that I couldn't speak to him because I was too ill. But she passed on his message saying that he was starting work on the design of the boat, and this was the best medicine I could have had.

Maureen couldn't spend her whole time looking after me. Our finances then meant that both of us had to earn what we could, and she had a job as a telephonist, which she could do while Samantha was at a nursery school. Maureen had had a few days' holiday over the New Year, but on January 5th she had to go back to work. I was a lot better by then, and able to do my own telephoning. And there was a lot to do – I had to find a builder for the boat, and also to deal with all the other little jobs of life, for ordinary life goes on even when the dream of a great adventure suddenly becomes real. Southern Television wanted me to go to their Southampton studio on January 7th to appear on one of their programmes, on January 8th I had arranged to give a lecture at Gerrards Cross, and so on and so on. I managed to keep both appointments (Maureen insisted that the television people sent a properly heated car to take me to and from the studio). I was lucky in Maureen's nursing, and in my pleurisy's having no complications.

I had, of course, to get back to my own job with Schweppes as soon as I was on my feet again, and every spare minute went in telephoning, writing, or going to see shipyards to find a yard which not only could build my boat in steel, but would guarantee to have the hull completed by July. This was a dreadful period – a word from a yard that it *might* be able to take on my boat would make me wildly elated, and the final answer that the job couldn't be done in time would plunge me into such despair that I felt the whole venture doomed to failure. Then I would take a grip on myself and say that whatever the seeming disappointments it was *just not going to fail*. I was determined to sail in the autumn of 1970. For one thing all my plans were based on this, for another I wanted to be the *first* to sail alone nonstop round the world from east to west, and if I were delayed – if my start had to be postponed for a year – someone else might get in ahead of me.

During this period both Maureen and I tried to keep diaries, and though the entries were often rather scrappy they do convey something of the worry and uncertainty that we lived through. Here are some extracts, starting from the time when I was still in bed with pleurisy.

January 2nd (Maureen). Drew up some lists on various points. Chay improving, but won't admit it – he is afraid I will stop pampering him if he admits he is a little better – Men! Now that the decision has been made by the British Steel Corporation it is gradually sinking into me that Chay is to be off once again. My feelings and thoughts are immaterial, but I shall be behind Chay whatever he contemplates. You can't stop a man from fulfilling his life – even if you think you can. My side is to keep our home full of happiness, welcome, enjoyment, and above all trust.

January 5th (Chay). Robert Clark phoned up with the basic measurements – 58–59ft overall, 8ft draught, 12ft 8ins. beam, $14\frac{1}{2}$ tons displacement. Some boat! Phoned Joyce Bros, boatbuilders – all booked up until August. Decided to try Vospers.

January 8th (Chay). Getting very worried about building the hull.

January 11th (Chay). Interview with Vospers arranged for Tuesday.

January 13th (Chay). Saw Vospers and explained situation. They were extremely charming and said they would do what they could, but told me not to stop searching for another builder. They asked various questions about the design which can only be answered by Robert Clark.

January 13th (Maureen). After Chay's interview with Vospers he went on to see Joyce Bros to ask Mr Joyce if it was possible for him to build the boat. Joyce Bros are piled high with work. A Canadian's boat is the next one to start. Mr Joyce gave us the Canadian's address and suggested that we wrote to him to ask if he would agree to a postponement of the start of the building of his boat. We wrote this evening – here's hoping.

January 17th (Chay). Went to London – Robert Clark ill in bed. I must remember always to phone up beforehand. Went round to Robert Clark's house and got answers for Vospers.

January 19th (Chay). Went along to Groves and Gutteridge in the Isle of Wight to ask about boat. There seems just a possibility.

January 21st (Chay). Letter from Terry saying he was trying to arrange a meeting with the chairman of Swan, Hunter.

January 22nd (Chay). Letter from Robert Clark asking one or two points. I must have a meeting with Terry – we haven't got the coordination sorted out properly yet. I'm now on sleeping pills – God, am I tired! It's really worry – I'll be OK once the hull is under way. I think of it almost continually. If anyone says this sponsor business is easy, they want to try it. Everything is a worry.

January 23rd (Maureen). Haggis supper. A night to remember. Very little discussed about boat, but quite a few points made about certain equipment necessary.

January 24th (Maureen). Awoke with a thunderous head. Six of us consumed $2\frac{1}{2}$ bottles of whisky, and tonight we have another haggis supper!

January 25th (Maureen). Both felt like death. Samantha was very sweet to us all day – somehow she understood.

January 26th (Chay). I just can't sleep. It's not the actual trip I'm worried about, it's in case it all falls through. When the hull starts I'm sure I shall feel a lot happier. I pray it is soon.

February 7th (Maureen). At noon picked up Samantha and drove to London. Appointment with Robert Clark at 3 PM. Chay received some drawings and talked to Robert about some alterations.

February 9th (Maureen). Chay started serious training

runs, exercises, etc. Training for Chay is a great morale booster.

February 21st (Maureen). Lecture by Miles Smeeton at the Royal Southern Yacht Club. We had to cancel going to the lecture as Chay had to rush off to Birmingham. Chay is worried about the lack of builders in steel with enough experience on small boats. It doesn't seem possible to be told that there is money allotted for a boat, and yet you can't get a builder to build her in the required time.

February 28th (Maureen). Chay had a meeting with Ron Amey, who has a large ocean racer. He has given permission for Chay to crew on board. This will give Chay experience in handling bigger craft, and also experience with the latest equipment. Chay is very pleased about this.

March 2nd (Chay). Well, we are now into March, and another disappointment. Groves and Gutteridge can't do it.

March 3rd (Maureen). What a day! I phoned up 29 builders from one end of Britain to the other, gave them the specifications and final date we could allow for it to be finished. Out of these, only six are possible, and I have to ring them again tomorrow after they have worked it out and decided whether they can meet the finishing date, etc. Most of them were put off when I told them it had to be finished by July 1st. That would give the rest of July for fitting out, and then six to eight weeks for trials. We have new hope – so that helps. I *know* one of them will take it and do it. We are just beginning Chay darling, you see!

March 4th (Maureen). I managed to get through to three of the six builders from yesterday. One wants me to send the plans the other two said no.

March 5th (Maureen). Philip and Son of Dartmouth think they will be able to do it.

March 7th (Maureen). Philip and Son have not given a definite answer, but it is 75–25 that they will do it.

March 11th (Chay). A very sad day – Vosper cannot do it. I phoned Dartmouth, and they *think* they can do it. Terry and I are to have lunch with Sir John Hunter of Swan, Hunter on the 17th. I don't really think they will do it, still, we'll see.

March 14th (Chay). Philip and Son say they can do it – what a relief!

March 17th (Chay). Had lunch with Sir John Hunter. He was most interesting and said he would see if he could help though he didn't think they could. I had to telephone him back at 5 PM and he said No go.

March 18th (Chay). British Steel Corporation approved Philip and Son as builders.

March 21st (Chay). Drove down to Dartmouth. What a super place – terrific atmosphere of boating. I spent $3\frac{1}{2}$ hours with the directors sorting out the problems. We eventually did sort things out.

March 22nd (Chay). Phone call from Robert Clark – drawings on their way to Philip and Son with enough work for two months. We're off!

March 26th (Maureen). Chay left for a weekend's sailing to France. They'll probably return on Monday. It will be a long holiday weekend on my own. I shall try to catch up on some little jobs that are outstanding.

March 29th (Chay). Just returned from Easter weekend to Cherbourg. I was in *Firedancer* of Hamble, Bill Cottell's boat, with Frank Allen, Willy, and David Dyer. It was super being on the water again. All the worries of the trip and everything else were forgotten, and I think I was completely relaxed.

March 30th (Maureen). This 'stag' Easter weekend seems to have given them all a new lease of life!

The euphoria did not last long. On April 2nd the yard at Dartmouth telephoned to say that everything was ready to lay the hull – but they hadn't yet received specifications for the steel plates. This meant telephoning Robert Clark – and we couldn't get hold of him on the telephone. I felt bitterly frustrated and upset.

I ought, of course, to have known better. Designing and building a boat the size of *British Steel*, especially when she has to be designed for such an unusual task as a single-handed voyage round the world, is an enormous and complicated job. I wanted everything to be done at once, and it just could not be. Take this question of steel, for instance – it had to be made and supplied to exact specifications in order to make the most of the strength-for-weight qualities possessed by steel, then it had to be tested, shot-blasted and treated against corrosion. There were endless opportunities for delay: that there were really very few delays is due solely to the magnificent teamwork between the British Steel Corporation, the shipyard, and the designer.

I was exceptionally lucky in the personalities involved in my project at the BSC. I have already recorded my debt to Mr W. F. Cartwright, the deputy chairman, and himself an experienced ocean-racing man. John Dunkley, the chief Press Officer, who was very directly concerned in my affairs, is a keen dinghy sailor, and Philip Wolfinden, a member of his staff, was yet another experienced small boat sailor. Phil Wolfinden, who has done a lot of offshore cruising, was given the job of coordinator of the whole project within the BSC. Everything went to him, and he dealt with the thousand-and-one problems that cropped up. When I was desperate, Phil was patient and understanding – and he got things done. I can never be sufficiently grateful to him and all his colleagues.

I tried to keep my mind off worrying by concentrating on my physical training for the voyage. I set myself a programme of daily runs, a short one in the morning and a longer one each evening. I cut down on food and sweeteners and tried to practise all the good training habits that I'd learned first in the Army.

April 24th was a great day. I wrote in my diary,

> Today at long last the talking's over. Now we know we're on our way. I phoned Philip's yard, and they said, 'We've got the steel for the hull and we've laid her.' This to me was like prayer. I booked a table at the Royal Southern Yacht Club so that we can have a wee dinner to celebrate. Soon the stuff will come in, and it will be flat out. The pressure and the worry really have been heavy, and it tells. It shows in your activities, words, and in the family. Both Maureen and I are a little highly strung and tense. We have a system for not getting 'ratty', and it works great. If we do get 'ratty' the same system makes it very short.

On May 9th I paid another visit to Dartmouth. I got to the hotel at 10.30 and by 11 I had unpacked, had a bath, changed and was in the car ready to go to the yard. That's one thing the Army teaches you to perfection – how to change quickly!

I turned a corner into the shipyard – and there it was, staring at me. To have been told over the telephone that the keel had been laid was magic; to see it was just magnificent. I just sat and looked. It had been hard work, but worth it. I felt sad that Maureen was not there to share that moment.

In the yard I had a long, close look at the keel, and thought that the workmanship was terrific. I had lunch with the chairman and directors of the yard, and the chairman said that they would finish on time. After lunch I was taken round the yard and met and chatted to a number of the men who were working, or who would be working, on my boat. They all seemed splendid people. As soon as I could I telephoned Maureen to give her all the news.

May 14th was my thirtieth birthday. Maureen wrote in her diary:

I got Samantha settled early, and Chay and I had a lovely candlelit dinner. We don't seem to have much time to spend together lately, so these special evenings I treasure. It doesn't seem possible that Chay is now 30 years old. When he woke this morning and realized he was now 30 it didn't go down too well. Samantha was terribly sweet, singing 'Happy Birthday, Daddy'.

After my birthday we gave ourselves a weekend in Wales. We left home about six o'clock on Friday evening and arrived pretty late, but we were up early the next morning and it was grand to be in the hills again. We had a good walk by Talybont, and for much of the way I carried Samantha on my shoulders, as the going was a bit rough for her. I wanted to test my fitness, and decided that, compared with the old days, I was really pretty unfit, and still overweight. When you live out of doors for a long period and are properly fit, you get a kind of aroma of fitness in your nostrils. That day I only got a sniff of it, but I felt that the real aroma would come.

On Sunday we packed picnic lunches and went for another long walk. The weather was glorious and we lay in the sun and slept. Both Maureen and I felt completely relaxed. But we had to get back to Portsmouth that night, and as we drove back we felt the tension building up again. We determined that we *must* try to relax more – but that's easier said than done. A few days later Maureen was writing in her diary:

Both Chay and I now seem like Zombies – we just automatically go on, mechanically, with no thought about tiredness. We *must* get some regular nights, or we shall crack up, and there will be no crew for *British Steel*.

My own diary gets scrappier and scrappier. I was still doing my job for Schweppes and somehow I had to fit in visits to London, to Dartmouth, to sailmakers, instrument makers, experts on rigging, and goodness knows how many other people, all directly or indirectly concerned with my voyage. Reading Maureen's diary now I realize how much she had to put up with, and how much I owe her. At the end of June, Maureen, who was still working as a telephonist, had a holiday, and she and Samantha went to Newcastle to stay with Maureen's mother. Before leaving Maureen wrote:

I am so much looking forward to my holiday – but it would be so much nicer if Chay and I could get away on our own for a few days. I am not going to ask, for I know that Chay has too much on his mind to have to worry about a wife who would like a few days' honeymoon. I must make a list of all the things I have to do while I am in Newcastle, quantities, manufacturers, etc. I think Chay is looking forward to our departure as much as we are. There are so many people he wants to see, and when we are at home he likes to spend as much time as possible with us, consequently neglecting some of the things he ought to attend to.

It now seemed fairly certain that *British Steel* could be launched in August and that I could set off on my voyage in October. The British Steel Corporation felt that it was time to make an official announcement about the project, and arranged a press conference at the Savoy Hotel in London on July 16th. I was naturally very much on edge, but we had a rehearsal the day before and it was less of an ordeal than I had feared. Mr Cartwright took the chair and people were very nice to me. A great many journalists came and we were asked about fifty questions, most of them good, searching and constructive. I was surprised at how technical many of them were. I had a great sense of relief in feeling that at last my project was 'official', that the world knew what I was trying to do and that I had no longer to be secretive, or half-secretive, about my plans.

I had had to make a decision about my personal life. All this time I was carrying on with my job as a representative for Schweppes, but it was becoming more and more impossible to do my job properly and to deal with all the preparations for my voyage. Reluctantly, for I liked the job and Schweppes had been good to me, I decided that I should have to resign, and I arranged to leave at the end of July. This was another worry, for it meant that I should no longer have an income, but there was nothing else to do.

Maureen had used her holiday in Newcastle to work out lists of all the food I should require on the voyage. Some was generously given to us by various manufacturers, the rest we had to buy ourselves. We had a very limited budget for this, and Maureen went to enormous trouble to ensure that it was well spent, to provide occasional goodies for me as well as all the basic essentials. We used our garage as a warehouse for all the stuff that was beginning to arrive.

In addition to my job and the work of fitting in appointments with people whose advice or help I needed for the voyage, I put in as much time as I could sailing in other people's boats. This was partly recreational, but, more important, it was a necessary part of my training and sailing education. I learned a lot about handling bigger boats than I'd been accustomed to, and I'm really grateful to the friends who let me crew for them.

Maureen's diary takes up the tale of those hectic weeks.

July 17th Chay travelled to Dartmouth early for the men starting work on the boat. Discussed points with Philip and Son and Robert Clark. Returned home late in the evening.

July 18th Took Samantha to the zoo as a pre-birthday treat, had birthday tea out. Evening spent working out remainder of clothing required for the trip.

July 19th (Sunday). Samantha's third birthday. The three of us went to Southampton and helped Eric Downey sail his 28-ft yacht to its new mooring. Managed to overhaul a 40-ft yacht (under sail only) into Portsmouth Harbour.

July 20th Both at work. A photographer and reporter came for interview for a Midland paper. Had early night. Chay restless, but now sleeping soundly.

July 21st Started sorting out charts and organizing which other charts will be required.

July 22nd Chay to Isle of Wight. I shall be glad when Chay is finished with Schweppes and can devote all his time to the present project. It is too much for him trying to do his best for Schweppes and arrange appointments with people for help with his trip.

July 24th Chay left early for Birmingham. Arrived home late. Lists sent to Brooke Bond and Oxo.

July 25th We all had a day off. Went swimming, had lunch out. Chay had a fitting at Gieves for a reefer jacket. I bought an outfit for myself, and one for Samantha, for the launching. Ordered polythene bags.

July 26th (Sunday). Chay came to Mass with us. Most of day and all evening spent dictating and typing letters. Early hours before we eventually put our heads on the pillow.

July 27th Garage prepared and cleaned for equipment.

July 28th Chay in discussion with David Russell. Returned very late. Spent evening doing all the things I haven't had time to do for some time, bath, nails, hair and generally coddled myself.

July 29th Chay overnight Isle of Wight. Typed out

chart numbers. Made programme of events until departure concerning boat. Still a great deal to do, but I am getting most things organized, knowing that once tins arrive I shall have very little time until varnishing is completed.

Maureen's note about varnishing may require a little explanation for those who have not stored small boats for long voyages. Tinned foods have paper labels on them, and paper does not last long in lockers which are bound to get damp even if they don't have seas swirling over them. In some circumstances, storing tins with paper labels on them can be dangerous, for the paper may come off and form a mass of sodden pulp, which can be sucked into pumps and block them at a critical moment. So all labels have to be taken off, and the tins varnished against corrosion. Once the labels are off, you do not know what a tin contains, so the tins have also to be marked with a code which tells you whether they are baked beans or strawberry jam. All this means a great deal of work, which Maureen gallantly took on. Her diary continues:

August 1st Went swimming. Paperwork, typing, my fingers are sore. Prepared and listed clothing for packing. Have taken over spare room for clothing, bedding, etc, that can't be kept in garage. At least the living-room at the moment is still clear.

August 3rd Went to *Anne of the 1000 Days*. Excellent film. Took me months to coax Chay, but eventually we made it.

August 4th Tested water-containers.

August 5th Chay went to Dartmouth to see progress on boat.

August 6th Chay Dartmouth. Met man from Marconi to arrange fitting, etc.

August 7th I gave up my job. Now real work on trip begins. Chay returned very late from Dartmouth.

I read this note in Maureen's diary with very mixed feelings. First comes admiration for her utter loyalty, but then I wonder what unspoken thoughts she must have had. I was asking an appalling lot from her. She is my wife, but she is also Samantha's mother – and mothers want secure homes for their children. What was I offering in the way of security? I was doing what I felt I had to do, and Maureen was backing me with everything she had. But from her point of view she was giving up, one by one, all the things that make for a woman's sense of security. It was a wonderful sort of trust. Her diary goes on:

August 9th Paperwork until after midnight.

August 11th Chay starting to worry about inadequate time for trials.

August 12th We went to London to see about compass and discussed different types. Ended up ordering compass as Robert Clark suggested. It looks very large and cumbersome. Nice relaxing lunch, all on our own. Returned in time to pick up Samantha from her nursery.

August 13th Took sextant to Southampton to be checked.

August 14th Dictation and typing all day.

August 15th Opened fete on Island. Came back to paperwork and lists of equipment and spares required. Lists are now pretty comprehensive, and I think about complete.

August 16th Last-minute details attended to before going to Dartmouth for the launch.

August 17th Departed early, arrived Dartmouth 10 A M. Chay went off to *British Steel* and spent the greater part of the day at the yard. I unpacked and went to Torquay with Samantha.

August 18th Spent all day at boat with Chay and helped where I could. Stayed out of the way when I wasn't required. Met many people at the yard. Returned to hotel to meet guests arriving for launching tomorrow. Sir Alec and Lady Rose were among the first to arrive.

British Steel was launched early in the morning of August 19th – that was the only time in the month when the tide would be exactly right for her. It was not a very convenient time, for it seemed to make it difficult to have a proper launching party, but the British Steel Corporation were wonderfully good about it, and in the end we had two parties – a pre-launch dinner overnight, and a champagne breakfast after the launching.

As the date of launching drew near I ought to have felt more and more excited, but instead I felt increasingly worried. I was very tired – would everything be all right, or would we, almost at this last hurdle, meet some unexpected, new delay? Four days before the launch my diary has this worried little note: Maureen left work as telephonist. No money. Keep bank manager in the picture.

The launch made up for everything. It was a fantastic day. About two hundred people came, and the launching ceremony was performed by Mrs Cartwright, the wife of Mr W. F. Cartwright of the BSC, who had been such a good friend to the adventure from the start. As she said 'I name this ship *British Steel*' the yacht seemed to hesitate for a moment, and then to make up her mind to enter her own element with confidence. She inched off the stocks and slipped into the water perfectly. It was a great moment, and *British Steel* looked absolutely beautiful as she sat gracefully on the water. I had to make a speech, and Maureen said that it was good, though I don't remember much about it. All I do remember is a feeling of complete thankfulness that we had come so far so well.

But there was still an appalling lot to do, and there could be no let-up in the pace of preparations. *British Steel* had to be rigged and fitted out, taken for trials, stored, and made ready for sea. The weight of paperwork and correspondence seemed to increase. I was constantly on the move, practically commuting to Dartmouth, having to go to London for all sorts of things, and visiting Peterborough to get instructions from the Perkins company on the diesel-engine installed in *British Steel* (not, of course, used for progress, but essential for generating purposes, a precaution for emergencies). In the middle of September Robert Clark, Phil Wolfinden, Frank Allen and Bill Cottell helped me to sail *British Steel* from Philip's yard at Dartmouth to Southampton for her final fitting out. After this things became a little easier, for I did not have to go to Dartmouth every time I wanted to do something on board. But not much easier – there seemed more and more to do and less and less time in which to do it. And I had to keep up my training programme, fitting in sailing practice by crewing on other people's boats whenever I could.

There were other things as well as training and preparing for the voyage. After much discussion Maureen and I decided to sell our house. She planned to go with Samantha to Newcastle to stay with her mother while I was away, and life after the voyage seemed so distant that it seemed sensible to sell the house. Also, we needed the money.

Maureen's diary tells the story.

August 20th Chay to Neville [Wood] to have a short revision course on some of the navigation. Letters and typing late. Late to bed, very tired.

August 21st Chay left for Cherbourg to assist Frank

[Allen] in bringing *Blue Crystal* back. I have started the varnishing – a dreadful job.

August 22nd Everywhere smells of varnish. Chay returned from Cherbourg at midnight. He decided to burn midnight oil and catch up on some outstanding correspondence. The Dictaphone certainly is handy. Chay is able to tape all his letters. Then when I have time, I type them.

August 23rd Chay and Frank left for Peterborough. Varnishing all day.

August 25th Varnished remainder of tins from Fray Bentos. Chay spent most of the day catching up on paperwork, spares, etc.

August 26th Chay London.

August 27th Chay to Portishead Radio, Somerset, to meet the technicians. Then on to Dartmouth.

August 28th Chay Dartmouth all day, returned late evening. Started sealing clothing and bedding.

August 29th Swimming and generally relaxed all day. Hope to devote all this holiday weekend to Samantha. Possibly last period of time we shall have together until Chay returns.

August 30th Left early for a picnic. Fabulous day.

September 1st Lots of food, etc is arriving now. Started making up 'special day' parcels.

September 4th Chay telephoned to say he is returning from Dartmouth tomorrow for the weekend. To be picked up at Salisbury. He did not seem too happy.

September 5th Samantha and I had a good journey to Salisbury, picked up Chay and then went and had lunch. Chay very downhearted. Everything not going too well. Still an awful lot to do on boat.

September 6th Caught up on a week's paperwork. My eyes and whole body seem terribly tired. Chay must feel exhausted with all these trips up and down from Dartmouth, and then worrying about boat.

September 7th Chay returned to Dartmouth and had a hellish journey (by train) taking nearly 6 hours.

September 8th Varnishing and preparing food.

September 9th Made a housewife for Chay – cotton, wool, needles, scissors, safety pins, etc. Cleaned up some rusty tools.

September 10th Cleaned up Calor gas stove and paraffin. Long, dirty job.

September 12th I could do with 36 hours in a 24-hour day. Heat-sealing, varnishing, typing all day.

September 13th Took Samantha to bathe. Relaxed doing some gardening.

September 14th Getting so tired unable to sleep. Everywhere smells of varnish. Chay, Robert Clark, Phil [Wolfinden], Frank [Allen] and Bill Cottell hope to leave today with *British Steel* for Southampton.

September 15th All arrived.

September 16th Cleaned and sorted out dental equipment ready to be checked by dentist. Bought Chay's Christmas and birthday presents. Must get some cards. Boat too heavy for Frank's mooring.

September 17th Chay to London – very tired and looks extremely pale. Phil [Wolfinden] with Chris Waddington took boat to mooring at Moody's.

September 18th All day spent at boat. Photographers at boat. Collected all Heinz food, which arrived at Royal Southern Yacht Club. Terry [Bond] helped to ferry home Heinz.

September 19th Prepared tins and varnished.

September 20th Varnished all day. Picked Chay up evening.

September 21st Chay to boat. House up for sale. All lists prepared and finalized.

September 22nd House sold subject to contract. Chay boat. Tension building up in house. Samantha very good.

September 23rd My arms ache with varnishing. Fantastic amount of work now completed. So much more difficult this time – Chay is not able to help me as he has so much to do on the boat. I am so tired I could sleep for a month.

September 24th British Steel is back and forward to Cowes. Rigging, etc. Chay very short-tempered. Samantha is getting too little attention.

September 25th Southampton, collected remainder of charts required and sextant from check.

September 26th Oh what a beautiful birthday! Chay sailing all day. Why am I so sentimental about birthdays, Christmas, etc? Samantha and I went to the cinema in the afternoon.

September 27th Typing all day. Heinz varnishing completed.

September 28th Pepsi cans all varnished. Gee whiz I ache!

September 30th Sir Alec [Rose] and Fred Cartwright out sailing with Chay. Place crammed with photographers and reporters. Amazing what a famous name and face does for newspapermen. Sir Alec gave Chay a lion made of rope and a lot of good advice.

October 1st Interior of *British Steel* looks good. Moodys have made bookcases, shelves, etc. Southern TV at 5.30. Took Chay's clothes to the boat and he changed at Moody's.

October 2nd Typing most of the day.

October 3rd Samantha and I went sailing aboard *British Steel*. What a fabulous boat! She sails like a dream – no wonder Chay is so pleased. Did sketch of interior to help loading and positioning for tins and boxes.

October 4th Everything is ready for loading, though it's

not possible to be completely ready – there will always be last-minute organized chaos, no matter how ready one is. Still odd bits of food arriving, and I varnish as they arrive.

October 5th Shopped for food – spent pounds.

October 6th Sealed sugar in polythene bags.

October 7th Chay left early for Southampton and Yorkshire Television filming. Met party and Chay at 2.00 for filming. Filmed afternoon and evening, including preparing and eating dinner. Exhausting day – terribly false, no matter how natural one tries to be.

October 8th Boat slipped (for anti-fouling, etc). Cash and Carry for remainder of food required.

October 9th Chay took lots of equipment to boat. Terry [Bond] took me with another load of equipment.

October 10th First batch of eggs collected, and prepared with petroleum jelly.

October 11th Most of day spent on boat. *British Steel* looks quite enormous out of the water. She is beautiful and looks so strong. Books and navigational aids on board.

October 12th Second batch of eggs delivered and prepared. Three loads of food taken to boat.

October 13th Boat all day helping with loading. Very tired.

October 14th Third batch of eggs (30 dozen) prepared and packed ready for trip. Ann Ingram transported load to *British Steel*. House gradually emptying.

October 15th British Steel back in water. Organized chaos trying to finish loading. Frank [Allen] working non-stop.

October 16th Binoculars presented to Chay. Doesn't seem possible that practically everything is on board – and it looks as if there will be a place for Chay as well! Compass swung after tins on board. Trim and final sail.

Dinner Royal Southern Yacht Club. Relaxing evening, enjoyed more than expected.

October 17th Boat blessed 4 PM. Chay extremely nervous, difficult to get him away from *British Steel*. Chay unable to relax and intends burning midnight oil. I think both Chay and I are pleased that the day has come for departure. Neither of us could stand many more days of the tension, pressures and sheer hard work that has been continuous over the past few weeks. Chay will be able to unwind a little in about 48 hours' time, when he should be leaving the congested shipping lanes.

A few hours after Maureen wrote this in her diary I was sailing out of the Solent on the first leg of my long voyage. It was Sunday, October 18th, 1970. I went on board *British Steel* from the jetty of the Royal Southern Yacht Club in the Hamble river, with Maureen and a small party of friends. We motored down the river to the starting area, near the Hook Buoy in Southampton Water, and there Maureen and my friends left me. They were taken off by *Blue Crystal*. I was alone for the first time and waiting for the starting gun, to be fired by Commodore A. R. Lightfoot of the RSthYC. Then the gun boomed across the water, and I was away.

People ask you what it feels like when you have cut the last links with home and family and realize that you are on your own – for nine or ten months at least, maybe for a year or more, perhaps for ever. The honest answer is that you don't feel anything. At that moment I think you are beyond feeling. You have a vague sense of thankfulness that something you have planned and worked and dreamed for has actually been achieved, and another sense that it's all make-believe, anyway, and you are still dreaming. But there isn't time to analyse your feelings, even if you could – there is too much to do. An armada of little boats carrying well-wishers,

press and television representatives, is milling around – you
need all your wits about you to keep out of their way. People
are sometimes rather thoughtless on these occasions. It is a
nice idea to sail out to cheer a lone voyager on his way, and
press and TV men have their jobs to do. But the lonely man
on board has been through a harrowing time, he is carrying
a load of anxiety, and it isn't fair to add to this by coming
close and crowding him. In one such mêlée just after my
start a launch hit *British Steel*, scoring a nasty dent in her
beautiful clean topsides. I was furious – it seemed so damned
unfair. And I thought, 'That's given me a quite unnecessary
extra job to do. I must get some paint on the scratch as soon
as I can or it will rust.' And I thought too, 'Thank God for a
steel boat. If we were wood or glass fibre that bash might
have been serious.' Ladies within earshot had their vocabulary increased by one word.

It was later, when I had time to think, that I realized what
an incredible amount of work had been achieved to make
the voyage possible. In January of that very year, *British
Steel* had not even been a line on paper. In just over nine
months she had been designed, built and fitted out for the
most taxing long voyage that any yacht has ever faced.
Often enough I was depressed and irritated with the builders
when some little thing went wrong, but really they did a
wonderful job. From the laying of her keel in April, *British
Steel* was built in just over four months. Keel-laying in
April, launching in mid-August – that must be almost a
record for British boatbuilding with a yacht of *British
Steel*'s size.

Reading Maureen's diary brings a lump to my throat. It
makes me feel dreadfully selfish – and I suppose I was. But
once the idea of the voyage took possession of me I *had* to
be selfish, or rather I had to set aside all thoughts of self – of
myself as well as Maureen – to concentrate on the one demanding task of getting *British Steel* built and getting ready

to sail. I drove myself hard. Did I drive Maureen? I did not do so consciously – I did not need to. She is so utterly loyal, so at one with everything in our life together, that she drove herself for me. I could not have succeeded without her. I think now that I must have come sadly near to straining even her loyalty – that she went on as she did is a tribute to her, not to me. She is an incredibly marvellous person. I can say only, Thank God for her.

CHAPTER THREE

But First – the Horn

I had head winds all that first evening of my voyage, and had to tack backwards and forwards. I was pretty exhausted when I left, and by nightfall I felt more like a zombie than a human being. I did what had to be done mechanically, but a bit of my mind kept thinking of the voyage ahead. If I could make it – well, it would be worth making. Not many of us in our lives can really hope to do something that has never been attempted before. Even my Atlantic rowing with John Ridgway was not something absolutely new – two New Jersey oyster fishermen had crossed the Atlantic in a rowing boat in 1897. This voyage on which I had now set out was something new in the world. No one before had ever tried a non-stop circumnavigation the way I was going, which was not just sailing from east to west; I had set out deliberately to sail, as it were, against the spin of the globe, to drive *British Steel* against the prevailing winds in the loneliest seas on earth. Oh well, I should meet what came as it came. I couldn't sit around and think of the future now, for the Channel is no place for relaxing. I helped to keep myself awake by putting in a radio-telephone call to Frank Allen.

I got through that first night somehow, and my second day at sea – October 19th – brought a kindlier wind. It helped me to make westwards towards the mouth of the Channel instead of forcing me to tack north and south as

I'd had to do during the night. I made a list of all the things that had gone wrong so far:

1. Sheared pin for self-steering gear.
2. Two tri-sail slides pulled out.
3. Cleat of handybilly pulled off.
4. One speedo not working (hit a log).
5. One light switch useless.
6. Two running hanks gone.
7. Mainsail shackle came adrift.

I put a wry note in my log, 'Not bad for 48 hours.' I was still landbound in my thinking – I hadn't got into my stride for the constant make-do and mend that is the lot of man on any small boat at sea. I was still nervy and on edge, but I felt a growing confidence in *British Steel*. I didn't particularly want to eat, and didn't feel like cooking; in any case, I didn't need to, for I still had bread and cooked meat from the 'first days' supplies that Maureen had carefully prepared for me.

On my second night at sea I made a link-call to Maureen by R/T. The radio-telephone is, of course, a boon to small boat sailors, and as a voyage goes on, the radio calls it enables you to make to people at home become the highlights of your life. But that first call to Maureen was strangely unsettling. I felt full of emotion, and very sorry for her. I seemed to have everything – first the excitement of planning, and then the carrying out of my great adventure. She had had months of desperately hard work – and suddenly, nothing. She was just left behind to clear up the mess of those months of preparation, and now she had to face the prospect of a year or so of being apart. I wanted to put my arms around her, and to try to explain how much I needed her.

The best cure for this sort of unsettlement is work. I got out a new set of charts, to take me from the Channel to the

Equator, and I began a great tidying up, to make things generally more liveable. On my third day I decided to cook some porridge. Making myself cook something probably did me good, but I can't say much for the porridge – it was awful. A great excitement on this day was a message from Portishead Radio saying that the Minister of Communications wanted to talk to me. I assumed that this would be a personal call from Mr Chataway, and I was so impressed that I put on a clean shirt in order to receive the call. But it turned out that the call was not from the *Minister*, but from some office in his *Ministry*, to arrange a schedule of R/T calls for me from the Falklands. I felt that this did not really merit a clean shirt, so I took it off and put on my old one again.

My log for Day 4 – October 21st – records:

First pause today for thought – my thoughts turn to Maureen and Samantha. Samantha will start to ask Mummy where I am – poor Maureen, Samantha is so insistent. I hardly saw her those past few days. It's going to be a bad year to miss in her life.

I could not, however, afford to be sentimental for long, for that fourth day brought what seemed at the time to be a disaster. I broke a running pole. This is a long metal pole for booming-out a headsail when running before the wind – it spreads the sail to catch the wind more efficiently. The break was serious, because it meant that I could not use my running sails to the best effect, and would have to suffer a loss of speed when running. The mishap did not altogether surprise me, I had been advised from the beginning by both Charlie Brooker and David Dyer that the booms should have had sleeves. I was not at all sure to what extent I could manage a repair, and I could not attempt repairs at once because there was quite a lot of wind, and the pole was dangerously awk-

ward to handle. *British Steel* was making about 6 knots
without a running pole and for the time being I had to be
content with that.

I still felt out of sorts and unable to settle down properly.
I think this was partly because I was not having regular
meals. My training told me that I should, but at that stage I
had no heart for cooking, and was still making do with the
bits of fresh food that I had. I determined that I must make
an effort and on Day 6 I had my first curry of the trip. My
goodness, was it hot! It almost burned my mouth off, but I
enjoyed it. The weather had been depressing, too, with
overcast skies that prevented my getting a sight to confirm
my position. Whether my hot curry helped to persuade the
sun to come out I don't know, but soon after I'd eaten it the
sun did come out. I got a sight, which put me at 43° 42′ N,
13° 30′ W. I had suspected that I was a bit both north and
west of the course I really wanted, and my sight confirmed
this. But I was not particularly worried, for it might have
been much worse. The sun also gave me a chance to dry
some clothes. I was helped at this time by feeling able to say
my first prayer of the voyage. It is, I suppose, easier to pray
when you are at peace with the world, and about this time I
began to feel something of the infinite peace that the sea can
give to man.

October 24th brought the end of my first week at sea.
I was getting over my initial unrest and beginning to settle
down. Work certainly helped: I had done a lot of tidying
up and *British Steel*'s cabin was not only shipshape
but even beginning to look a little homely, with photographs of Maureen and Samantha taped above the chart
table.

I had my first go at cooking chips – it took me two hours
to peel and cook them, and even then they wouldn't turn
brown. When I did finally eat them they were as hard as hell.

I thought how much better (and quicker) a job Mauree⟨n⟩ would have made of it.

My first rendezvous of the voyage was to be off Madeira and I expected to be there in four or five days. I should have made it in four, but a silly error in working out a sight cos⟨t⟩ me the best part of a day. I was working on the figure⟨s⟩ when a radio call from Frank Allen came through. I wante⟨d⟩ to give him my position because he was due to meet m⟨e⟩ with Anthony Thomas of Yorkshire Television, at th⟨e⟩ rendezvous off Madeira. So I went on working out th⟨e⟩ figures while talking on the radio, and the result was that ⟨I⟩ drew the intercept 'towards' and not 'away' as it should have been. And I not only gave Frank a wrong position, but worse, I altered course on it, which took me well to the wes⟨t⟩ of Madeira before I discovered my mistake. I comforte⟨d⟩ myself with the well-known saying, 'Things are seldom a⟨s⟩ good, or as bad, as first reported'. Then I had a bath and ⟨a⟩ complete wash and shave, and felt much better for it.

Our rendezvous was for the purpose of handing over ma⟨il⟩ and film which I had been taking on board for television⟨.⟩ My voyage had to be singlehanded and non-stop, whic⟨h⟩ meant that I could not put in anywhere on the trip for sup⟨-⟩ plies, repairs, or anything else. But the rules did permit m⟨e⟩ to receive letters, or to give mail and film to passing ships⟨,⟩ provided that no one actually came on board *British Steel*⟨.⟩ I'd been given detailed written instructions on the camera⟨s⟩ and radio equipment for TV, and I spent a long time tryin⟨g⟩ to work out how best to take photographs of myself doin⟨g⟩ things about the yacht. I had a lot to do before the firs⟨t⟩ rendezvous.

October 27th was a bloody day – it started with tw⟨o⟩ poached eggs and ended in complete exhaustion. I had no⟨t⟩ yet managed to repair my broken running pole, which mean⟨t⟩ that I had only one usable pole left. This, in turn, meant tha⟨t⟩ I had to change the pole from port to starboard, or vic⟨e⟩

versa, whenever I wanted to tack with a boomed-out sail. On that day I had to change my boom to port. I started at 10.00 hours and the job took me until 11.45. The halyard got all tangled up. I had it hoisted three times, and each time had to drop it because of a foul-up. Then I had to take down the main, because I was running under foresail. The main wouldn't come down. After much struggle I went aloft, got halfway up the mast and saw the trouble. Down I came, for the necessary tools, then back up – I was up the mast for over an hour, and that was no joke. In the course of things the main shackle bent to such an extent that it had to be replaced, but I couldn't do it at once because I'd pulled a muscle in going up the mast and had to rest for a bit. All this takes little enough time to read, but my trips up and down the mast and struggles with the gear took me the entire day – it was 22.15 hours before I was through.

The next day went a good deal better. I was comforted by noticing how fresh a sprig of white heather (given to me by my sister Jean) still looked. I had put it over the chart table, and it seemed to cheer up the whole chart-space. On this day I started saying grace before a meal. This is something that I think all families should do – we are jolly lucky to be able to have meals, and we really ought to be grateful.

I made the rendezvous on October 29th. My log recalls:

A joyous day – a sad day! I rendezvoued with Frank and Anthony just off Madeira at 09.15 hrs. In fact, it should have been earlier, but there were a lot of fishing boats when we reached the RV and it was still dark, so we missed each other. It was great to see them. We talked for an hour – they were in a dinghy put over from the boat they were on. It seemed stupid that they couldn't come aboard – still, that's the way it is.

We exchanged letters, from Maureen and to Maureen. I passed over the films, and also my logs to date.

After they had gone I set sail for the SW. It left me feeling very depressed and full. I read Maureen's letters and was moved even closer to her. We are fortunate in being spiritually together. I remember going to church in Bahrein (in 1964) and knowing that she would be in church on the same day.

I had to have a few hours' sleep – I felt very tired, more from mental than from physical work.

With her letters, Maureen had sent some tapes recorded by herself and Samantha, which I could play back on my tape recorder. To hear their voices was a joy, and I blessed them both.

The first week of November brought mainly pleasant weather and fairly gentle sailing. I was in the latitudes to which people go for winter holiday cruises, and although my singlehanded voyage was scarcely a holiday cruise at least I could enjoy some holiday weather. I decided to give myself a Happy Hour every day – one hour during which I would try to relax and deliberately do things that I enjoyed doing. I celebrated my first Happy Hour with my first whisky of the trip, drunk with American Dry (Schweppes of course!). I had one whisky only and it was quite enough – I don't drink much at sea. I enjoyed reading Georgette Heyer's *Friday's Child*.

My main task was to try to mend my broken running-sail boom. I'd radioed a description of the break to Phil Wolfinden and he'd sent back a message of technical advice from the makers. It would have been easy enough to carry out in a well-equipped workshop on land, but handling a 25-foot pole was a different matter singlehanded on a small boat at sea. But I did as well as I could. I could make a repair only by shortening the pole, from 25 feet to just over 22 feet. This interfered with the set of the running sails, but it was better to have a shortened boom than none at all. The job suddenly became urgent because my remaining running boom went. It was in the early hours of the morning, and I was comfortably asleep, with *British Steel* moving along happily in light airs. There must have been a sudden gust for I was awakened by an almighty bang. I rushed on deck, and, sure enough, it was the remaining running boom broken.

Though the weather was pleasant I was not pleased with my progress (partly the fault of those wretched running booms). My log records feelings of frustration and depression:

November 2nd Calms – Force 1. What a drag of a day – have done nothing all day except try to keep her going. Just calms and zephyrs of a breeze. This is the time when it gets me worst – sun shining, and sails just banging back and forth. This is not a fast passage. Could mean mid-January at Cape Horn – that's not so good, but let's wait and see. Finished Nevile Shute's book *Trustee from the Toolroom*. Surprised not to see some ships – I'm reasonably close to the Great Circle course. So far I've only seen ships at night. Curry for dinner, with rice. Also had whisky (Happy Hour).

November 3rd Light winds, Force 1–2, NE. This has been the worst day so far – I really felt very depressed. Why? Well, I suppose it's due to the calms and light winds – I never could stick them. I tried to fix the other boom, but no go. I don't have another section that size. I also fixed the forehatch – it would close, but wouldn't lock. Next I extended the strap 'keep-in' for the galley. Then I tried to get the Zenith going – not very good reception. This is because I haven't really fully understood the instructions. I fitted an external aerial to it – this makes a great deal of difference. I'm sure all will be well. I've been playing some tapes, but unless I

concentrate I find I'm out of hearing distance. Also gave
self-steering gear a going over.

The next day – my eighteenth at sea – brought a bit of
wind and *British Steel* began to slip along at 6 knots. I had a
haircut, wash and shave, and that helped to cheer me up. I
gave myself a vegetable curry for dinner, and it should have
been a good day except that I suddenly began to worry
about getting ill. This is an anxiety that comes to all singlehanded sailors and you have got to be firm about it. At the
same time you have got to try to be sensible, for if there is
anything seriously wrong you owe it to your family to try to
get medical help as soon as you can. I began feeling a pain in
my right side – was it anything, or nothing? I worried about
it off and on for the rest of the day, and tried to take my
mind off it by starting a Linguaphone course in French that
I'd brought with me.

On November 5th I spoke again to Maureen via Portishead Radio. My log for that day gives an indication of my
feelings, and also records some of the worries that are in-
separable from a long voyage alone.

November 5th 07.00 GMT spoke to Portishead to
Bruce Maxwell [a reporter then on the *Sunday Mirror*],
and Phil Wolfinden. Gave them details of last week's
events. Afterwards I spoke to Maureen and heard Samantha. It was great hearing them both and knowing that
all is well. Maureen says not to worry about them, but I
can't help worrying. It's not as if she was flush. I know she
will get a job – goodness knows, a lesser woman would
crack. She is my strength in times of desperation – I draw
on her strength. I have only to pray, and somehow all the
family are very much closer, and I always feel refreshed
for it.

Took some photographs today. Doing basically

nothing. I'm trying to tune myself to the situation down at
the bottom [round Cape Horn] and formulate a new plan.
Originally I was going to the east of the Island de Los
Estados [Staten Island], now I think I'll go between
[through the Le Maire Strait that separates Staten Island
from Tierra del Fuego]. Suppose when it comes to it, I'll
play it off the cuff.

Good sailing day – first time the speedos have been at
10 knots since I started. Found a flying-fish on deck –
dead, poor soul.

23.30 hrs. Well, the running-boom has gone again – not
at the repair I made, but at the weld. What a bloody
carry on! What worries me now is the mast – my
confidence in its staying in one piece is slowly going. All
the time now I know I mustn't chance it, and I'll have to
play safe to get round. At the end somebody will say,
'Why didn't you drive the boat harder?' I'll clout the bas-
tard. All along the plan was to go absolutely flat out,
aiming at 150 miles average a day. That would mean less
than 12 months. Now, with the booms broken, and all at
the weld, how, honestly, can I? I really am furious.

The failure of those booms hit me in two ways. There was
the direct effect on speed – when *British Steel* was running I
could not hope to make the speed she could have achieved if
the booms had been intact. And there was the indirect effect
on me – failure of any one important piece of gear inevitably
made me fear for the rest. As the mast continued to stand up
I gradually lost my fear of a break but nevertheless it was
always at the back of my mind and tempted me to play for
safety when I really wanted to keep going as fast as I could. I
managed to repair the running boom again, but the sail
never set as well as it would have done with a full-length
boom. I just had to make the best of it.

I now had to face the Doldrums, that belt of calms, rain

squalls and variable winds that lies near the Equator between the north-east and the south-east trades. I was then about 11°N of the Equator, and (with luck) I could hope to pick up the south-east trade wind somewhere between 8° and 60°N. On the other hand I might not – I might have to get as far as 2°N. In the days of sail ships were sometimes lucky and romped through the Doldrums in a day or so – if they were unlucky, they could be becalmed for weeks. Here are some extracts from my log.

November 9th Wonderful day's sailing, slipping along between 6 and 9 knots. The wind has gone up and down, also had a rain squall. Getting near to Doldrums, but should pick up the SE trades about 8°N. It really has been a glorious day. I did some doby [washing]. Also cleaned the doghouse – it was all covered in soot from charging the batteries. BBC Radio 2 gone. Can't grumble – managed to get it this far, which really is very good. Now I'm on to the World Service for time signals and news, using the Zenith. It's going to be a real godsend, that radio. Last lot of potatoes gone. Also discovered 16 packets of cheese – they had all gone off, so had to throw them away. But still other stuff left. Great lunch – two Guinnesses, cheese, crackers, onions and garlic – Boy, was I ill later!

November 10th Day's run 160 miles. Not sure, but *may* be through the Doldrums. What a night last night, full of squalls and rain and lightning. I was up all night, I hope that's the end of them. If there's nothing tonight then I think I'll be through, though I'm only at 9° 25'N.

03.00 hrs. Now I know I'm *not* through the Doldrums – all night it's been squalls. It's very frightening – you get very little warning except the big black clouds and the shimmering on the horizon. Then rain, wind, lightning all together. Your choice – reduce sail or run before it.

Saved 17 flying fish lives – was even hit on the back by one of them.

November 11th Day's run 180 miles. We've been reaching all day at a steady 7–9 knots. Only once did I have to drop the mainsail for a squall. But I'm in for another night of squalls – there's a lot of lightning about. At home and on land I never worry about lightning but at sea it's terrifying how it lights up the whole area round you. I draw strength from prayer.

Not sure yet, but I *think* I've met the SE trades. I shall be delighted to get away from these squalls. There was one very bad one, and I was due to go through it – it was as black as hell. I thought 'not funny', and altered course to go off wind of it and so pass it. Who's a coward? So I'm a coward.

November 12th I couldn't get a sight today because of overcast. I'm hoping for an accurate position because the wind changes force and direction so much. Not sure what has made me feel like this, but really depressed. Barometer dropping.

November 13th 2° 18′N, 27° 40′W. Still I'm being pushed towards the coast [of Africa] but according to the books the wind will gradually swing to the east the farther south I go. Had more squalls last night, with one which could only be described as a King Squall.

I'd had a couple of hours, and woke at 03.00. I went outside into the cockpit, and surrounding me was a great blanket of black cloud. My first reaction – get some sail down. At this stage the wind was about 15 knots. No sooner had I thought about it than – wham! 40-knot wind, and rain screaming across us. I had to fight, but eventually got us running downwind. I then ran forward to get the main down – halfway down it jammed, and *British Steel* came on the wind again. I left the main flapping like mad, got her downwind, then back to the main and eventually got it down. All the time the rain beating at me – I was completely starkers, and slipping without even shoes on. As soon as it had passed and the wind was back to 15 knots, up main! The rest of the night was spent in *reasonable* squalls, 25–30 knots.

Listened to the Merchant Navy Programme – always do at sea. Jean Challis is very good. Might write in a request myself one day – wonder where I'd post it?

Saw a ship heading N – probably came from S America. Started taking my vitamin pills – today is the second time. Curry for dinner tonight – that's about the seventh in a row. I've plenty of alternatives – it's just that I curry the alternatives.

On November 14th I crossed the Equator, at 13.45 GMT, about twenty-eight days – to the hour – from starting. I crossed at Longitude 28° 8′W. Then I turned slightly to the west. I had nothing special in the way of celebrations – there was really nothing to celebrate, merely that one minute you are in the northern hemisphere, the next in the southern. I remembered that the last time I crossed the Equator I had been with Maureen, in *Dytiscus*, and I threatened to throw her in. We had a good day and a wee celebration. I was sad that she was not with me now. I felt myself missing her and Samantha very much, so I gave myself some jobs. I greased the rudder and sorted out some stores. I thought that *British Steel* was rather too heavily loaded forrard, so I shifted stores aft to raise the bow a bit. I changed to my next packet of charts – Equator to Cape Horn.

Next day I got out my navigation books and re-read everything I had relating to the rounding of Cape Horn. The mariner has two choices for the passage. The tip of South America curls eastwards, and off the easterly end of Tierra del Fuego there is a biggish island, about sixty miles in length. This is Staten Island (or Island de Los Estados) and

it is about 150 miles north-east of Cape Horn. Staten Island
is separated from the mainland of Tierra del Fuego by the
Le Maire Strait, which is about as wide as the English Channel between Dover and Calais, twenty miles or so across.
That does not give much sea-room in bad weather, but if
you can go through the strait you don't have to go round
Staten Island. This is a considerable short-cut, saving at
least 60 miles of beating, maybe more if you are unlucky
with the wind. So the choice is – the short cut through Le
Maire, or the long way round Staten Island? The trouble is
that navigation in the strait is horribly tricky. There is a 5-
knot current, and if the wind is over tide conditions are
liable to be highly dangerous – *Ocean Passages of the World*
informed me that even a well found large ship could be
damaged. Moreover, you have also to find your strait; and
an entrance twenty miles across is a small target after some
7,000 miles without a landfall. Naturally I wanted to save
time by taking the short-cut, so I did my homework about it
very thoroughly. But I couldn't determine whether in fact I
should be able to use the strait until I got there and saw what
the weather was like. But I would be unable to go through
with a southerly wind.

I felt that I had been, perhaps, a little rude to the Equator
in having no celebration when I crossed it, so I stood myself
an Equator Dinner, one day late. The menu was tinned ham,
salad and mushrooms washed down with vin rosé. Not long
afterwards I had a visitor – some kind of seabird, but it was
not like a gull. It was greyish-black in colour, with a white
patch on the forehead. The bird was about fourteen inches
long and stood about eight inches high; it had webbed feet,
and a long, curved beak. It hopped down into the saloon,
but after it had done its business a couple of times I put it
back on deck. I took a number of photographs of it, and
then it tried to bite me. I offered it flying fish, biscuits and water, but no go – it didn't seem to want to eat. It

stayed with me for about twenty-six hours, and then, as if
it felt that it had rested long enough, it took off and
went. I was sorry to see it go, and hoped that it might come
back.

When my bird went I thought I'd cheer myself up by
listening to the radio. I'd have done well to be content with
solitude, for I got a news broadcast which told me that

1. Approximately a thousand people had died in a hur-
ricane in Pakistan.

2. Seventy-five had died in an air crash in the USA.

3. Fourteen people had been killed in Vietnam.

4. The Church was having another go at South Africa.

5. Arab liberation threatened Israel (again).

6. Israel was giving out an equal statement.

My log adds the note, 'When people ask, Do you listen to
the news, the answer is Not very often.'

I was not far off the coast of Brazil, about seventy miles
east of Recife, and I began to see some ships. I was glad to
come on the shipping lanes, for it served as a check on my
navigation, but it also meant no sleep at night, for with other
shipping about I had to keep a careful watch. It was safer by
day, when other ships should be able to see me, so while I
crossed the shipping routes I slept by day and stayed on
watch all night. I reckoned that I had to cross about 600
miles of sea to be clear of the shipping routes again. Some
jottings from my log at this time:

November 19th Interesting day – I've seen five ships,
and all only a matter of a couple of miles away. I'm surprised none has come across, purely out of curiosity from
the nautical side. But I suppose they see all they want
from binoculars. Two very big whales passed close. I'd no
time to get a decent picture, only distant ones. It took me
a few moments to realize what they were – when I saw the

great splashes my first thought was a bank or breaker. Don't like them getting too close.

Thought of my mother and childhood a lot today. I've been very fortunate in life – very happy childhood, close family, wonderful time at school, then 9 years in the Regiment. My greatest fortune was marrying Maureen, and now to have my daughter Samantha Fiona. How sad it would be to die now: but I don't think I will, not on this trip, anyway. I feel that I shall get home safely.

November 20th Dolphins visited me in the night. They cross and recross in front of the bow, playing. I flash the torch on them and it gives them a real fright. You should see them move away from the torch but they always come back until they get bored.

November 21st In three days I've had about 8 hours' sleep. It's a great effort to keep awake. But I mustn't sleep at night because I'm in the shipping lanes, and I get very little sleep during the day because I'm always at the tiller or adjusting the running gear.

I suffered bitterly from those wretched running booms. The wind at this time was mostly from the north-east, and my south-westerly course meant running dead before it. But with only one boom – the one I'd managed to repair – I could run dead before the wind, but I would suffer from chafe so I kept it on one quarter. This meant tacking downwind, and with only one boom I was constantly having to shift it from side to side. Moreover, when the wind was light I had to be perpetually at the tiller, for when running in light airs there was not enough wind pressure on the vane of the self-steering gear to activate it properly. If the booms hadn't let me down and I'd had decent running gear, the sails would have held my course before the wind, and I'd often have been doing 8–9 knots instead of having to sail at round 6 knots. I felt badly let down, but apart from the booms I couldn't grumble at *British Steel*. She was proving a beautifully balanced boat, and I grew to love her more and more.

After those frustrating light airs I soon had trouble. I wasn't expecting it, for the books say that the frequency of gales in this area is rare, but I had a gale all the same. The wind began to get up in the night, and by morning it was blowing Force 5. I still had the main and running sail up – over 1,000 square feet of sail, but trusting in the recorded infrequency of gales I felt sure that the wind would soon go down, and ignored the barometer (fatal mistake). By 08.00 it was blowing around Force 7 and it was high time to get the running sail down. When it was halfway down one of the self-steering gear lines broke – it couldn't have been better timed to make things difficult if someone had cut it. I was running back and forth trying to steer and get the sail down at the same time. But *British Steel* did her best to help me – she is so well-balanced.

Next, the main had to come down – and it stuck. I simply couldn't shift it, and after half an hour of trying it was still stuck, half up, half down. I prayed, and asked for strength and assistance – at my next try, down it came. I wrote in my log:

> No one will ever say to me that there is no God without my remembering all these situations. To atheists I say, Go sailing singlehanded for a few weeks.

The weather stayed rough all day, and the night that followed was absolutely black – until all of a sudden the whole sky was lit by streaks of lightning. That lightning went on and on, flashing all over the place, sometimes directly overhead. It was a fierce electrical storm, and I felt terrified. Surrounded by lightning alone at sea you can't help wondering what, apart from the boat, there is for lightning to strike.

But that storm passed, and then the wind swung all round the clock. In one period of twenty-four hours I changed sail twenty-one times, including setting and unsetting the mainsail four times. I was still not very far from the South American coast and a land bird alighted on the mizzen crosstrees. He stayed for about half an hour. A number of moths also came on board. There were some huge ones, reddish in colour, with a wing-span of about four inches; they were hideous. There were also some little ones, in bright fancy colours.

On November 24th the wind headed me, blowing directly from where I wanted to go. My log continues:

November 24th Not to worry – I'll get there some time. It's blowing about Force 5 now – the book says gales are rare, but have been known! (Evening) It's now Force 7 – so much for the book.

I'm not really at all happy with the rig. The trisail has to be shackled on to a slide, but the shackle moved and the slide jammed – must think of another way. The sheets for the No 3 jib are too short – thank goodness Ben gave me plenty of spares. Went up to crosstrees to see where the slides are jamming. Couldn't see anything but from below it looks as if the track protrudes slightly where the mainmast is riveted at the crosstrees.

I may sound as if I'm moaning – I'm not really. If we'd had a month of hard weather we'd have found all this out – I'll get it fixed. I'm getting over the problems as they arise.

I hit something last night – it was big; sounded rather like a fifty-gallon drum, or it could have been five gallons. Whatever it was it gave a hellish bang. Can't see any damage. Have to wait for a calm to go over the side.

November 25th Position 20° 55′S, 39° 17′W. Thought I was farther south than that, but with these light winds and continuous tacking it is easy to lose thirty miles in three days (last time I took a sight). That's only 10 miles a day – not bad, considering going back and forth like a yo-yo.

Had wash and shave. Studied my face for about half an hour. Decided I'm looking older, definitely older.

Had a visitor, a big gull, not quite as big as a wee albatross, but big. Very snobby – threw him some biscuit, but no go.

At present I'm heading SE. The wrong way – but it's good practice!

November 26th Buenos Aires Radio tried to contact me, but couldn't receive me. Next Portishead Radio – I had them clear as a bell, but just couldn't get through.

Flat calm again. I edge south at about 3 knots, a big difference from 8 knots. It's sent all my calculations haywire, and I still have head winds.

Saw a ship, and it was stopped. I was headed almost directly for it on my westing tack. Every so often great belches of smoke would come out of her, and she would go forward. I got within about two miles. If I'd got there, I was going to offer the Captain a tow. He'd have loved that!

At the top of the mast I have my wind vane and speed cups. The mounting has come loose, so up the mast I went. I haven't got a screw that fits – would you believe it? I have hundreds of nuts, and not one to fit. I'll have to go back up and lock it down with wire or something. Hope I don't lose it in the meantime.

Lunch – pears and cream. I've been at the tiller almost all day, trying to get the best from what little wind there is.

November 27th I'm so excited, just like a wee boy! First, contact with Portishead Radio on 12 m/cs. On the radio for an hour. These blokes work hard, far from just sitting at a radio. I was shattered after an hour, so what must it be like after a day? You have to re-tune every so often, spell words out, repeat words. They work wonders to get me all this distance – and I can't even get Buenos Aires.

Next, some wind came. Not much, but some – *and it's from the SE*! I move about ever so carefully in case I should frighten it away. It's only Force 2, but it's better than Force 3 in the wrong direction.

I was at the tiller almost all of last night. Now I'm going to have a couple of hours' sleep.

My Great Circle course to the Horn – that is, my course on the shortest curved line across the earth's surface – was now 2,000 miles. To follow it, however, I should have had to sail fairly close to the South American coast. The passage books recommend keeping about 100 miles offshore. To do so would add about 400 miles to the Great Circle distance, but I decided to follow the recommended course, and keep offshore. I should be able to carry more sail, and, with luck, it should be a more profitable course for wind.

I spent all my spare time reading up passage-notes and making calculations. So far things had gone pretty well, but I was conscious of the really testing time that would come when, as I put it to myself, we 'turned the corner'. The barometer was falling, and it looked as if we were in for a long, hard blow. I was thankful that we were still running, and not on the wind. I knew that I should have more than enough flogging to windward later on.

The blow came, with the wind gusting at about Force 7 and rain coming down in bucketfuls. I collected some ten gallons of rainwater for washing: it was nice to have fresh water to wash in, but I wasn't worried about water for I still had over 100 gallons on board. Visibility got very poor in the rainstorms, and at times was not much more than 100 feet or so. I spent a couple of hours standing on top of the cockpit, just leaning against the mast, and looking at things. With visibility as poor as it was there wasn't much to see, but the ever-changing moods of the ocean somehow absorbed me. I sang 'The Road and the Miles to Dundee' at the top of my voice. With so much rain and wind around I don't think there was even a seabird in the audience.

I was now in an area of particularly difficult sailing. To reach the Horn I had to get south and west, but there was a current against me, tending to push me east, and I could expect a good many head winds. I could also expect squalls, those sudden fierce gusts blowing off the Argentine pampas that are called 'Pamperos'. The wind that came with the rain – although rough, it had been a good one – held for some twenty-four hours, and then it fell calm. On November 30th – my forty-fourth day at sea – I covered just twenty-one miles. It was a miserable day's run, and worse, it had required a lot of tiresome work, for nursing the yacht in light airs meant being at the tiller most of the time.

My first Pampero caught me unexpectedly, and I was angry with myself, for all the books had warned me of Pamperos. I had all the signs – and neglected them. The barometer fell from 1007 to 1004 and I ought to have been on my guard, but the squall came so suddenly that it seemed to come out of nothing. The wind got up to about 40 knots and it hit us so hard that it bent the tiller slightly. I made up my mind not to be caught again.

That, however, was a resolution easier made than kept. The next Pampero hit me so suddenly that I didn't even have time to get out of the cockpit to reach the mainsail. One moment the wind was blowing at about 25 knots, the next at 55 knots – around Force 10. It lasted only a few minutes, and then dropped to about 35 knots. That was too much for the full main and I tried to get it down, but my luck was out and again it stuck. I had a fearful struggle to get it in, and I hurt my elbow rather badly by banging it on a winch.

I was seriously worried by the jamming of the mainsail. I needed to be able to set and hand it quickly, for the squalls came so suddenly that I could be caught out dangerously if I couldn't drop the main when a fierce one came. To play safe and keep the main reefed or down between the squalls meant losing speed, and I couldn't afford to lose speed because I couldn't risk delay in rounding the Horn. I was a bit late as it was – if I lost much more time I'd be meeting Cape Horn seas at a bad time of year. I radioed Phil Wolfinden for advice on the jamming, but I couldn't always make contact to receive messages. While waiting for his reply I had to do what I could on my own.

I spent one whole afternoon trying to discover the *cause* of the jamming, but the only thing that really came to light was that I couldn't climb the mast wearing an oilskin suit – it didn't give me enough freedom of movement! When, in more suitable clothes, I did go up the mast I couldn't find much wrong, except – as I'd seen from the deck – that the mainsail track seemed to be protruding slightly. I sandpapered every little roughness I could see, poured on masses of lubricant and hoped for the best.

In England, though I did not then know it, Phil Wolfinden was going to enormous trouble, first to get me the fullest possible technical advice on anything that might be wrong with the main halyard block or the sail track, and then to ensure that his radioed advice should reach me. He wrote by airmail to Mr T. Van de Velde, the Marconi representative in Buenos Aires, sending him a copy of the message and asking him to do everything he could to make sure that I got it. Mr Van de Velde was a good friend. He wrote back to Phil at once saying that the Buenos Aires station, Pachecco Radio, had been trying to contact me, but that although it had called on three different frequencies it had been unable to raise me. He added that the radio station would continue to listen out for me daily, and wrote, 'You must rest assured that I and the local radio station will do all we can to get your message to Chay Blyth.'

I find it very moving now to recall the many different people in different parts of the world who worked so hard to help me. I was one human being alone in a lonely ocean, but through my radio I had a host of friendly helpers. That I couldn't always get through to them just when I wanted was the natural lot of seamen. I was lucky to have the radio, and lucky to benefit from all the experience that has gone into these small Marconi sets since Chichester proved that they could work across the Atlantic in 1962. I shall always be grateful to my known and unknown radio friends. I did get Phil's message – and it was but one of many useful messages from him that helped and encouraged me throughout this voyage. I worked hard on the halyard block and track in the light of Phil's advice, and although I had trouble again later I was certainly able to improve things for a time.

The Pamperos continued to hit the yacht. One in particular really scared me. The wind was from the south and I could see the squall coming. Suddenly the deck was besieged by thousands of small moths and cobwebs magically appeared in the rigging. I was bemused by them. I just stood there intrigued, thinking that I had read somewhere about this phenomenon. Too late I remembered that the moths and the cobwebs are a certain warning of a bad squall in this area. There was no time to lower the sails. The squall hit with appalling force. I could hardly see but a quick squint at the wind speed indicator showed 60 knots.

The yacht was laid over on her beam ends. I kept talking to myself, giving myself instructions, saying, 'Luff up, luff up, Chay.' The mainsail, which I'd left untied, was flapping madly, and I heard everything crashing down below. Getting her round to go downwind was no joke. However, after a couple of minutes I managed it, and it made an agreeable change (although, of course, it was in the wrong direction).

No sooner had I done all this than the wind dropped to about Force 7. I didn't want to lose miles by running backwards, so I put her round and we were hard on the wind again. That particular Pampero did one odd thing – it straightened the tiller which an earlier squall had bent!

I had a sad supper that evening. I'd intended it to be a good one, with a menu of pastry, braised celery (*British Steel* style) and roast potatoes – but I forgot about the potatoes and they got burnt.

It was getting bitterly cold, and I took to sleeping in two sleeping bags, one inside the other. Checking over my stores I made an unpleasant discovery – Maureen and I had underestimated the number of boxes of matches I should need on the trip, and if I went on using matches as I had been using them, they wouldn't last out. I decided to ration myself to not more than five matches a day. This was not exactly hardship, but it was a nuisance.

I fought hard to make westing, and it paid off. I got a longitude sight at 18.00 GMT on December 14th, and it put me smack on the 100-fathom line. I checked with the depth gauge a couple of hours later, and it showed 60 fathoms. I treated myself to a whisky – the first for a long time – and chicken for dinner. That dinner, though, was marred by a disaster. I'd got only nine bottles of grapefruit juice left, and I thought I'd have one of them. I went aft to get it, and put it on a shelf while I closed the locker. *British Steel* rolled, and the bottle fell and broke. I was furious with self-pity.

My eyes were sore with going to windward; spray was constantly hitting them, and they were red with repeated rubbing. I gave myself some relief by bathing them with fresh water. Some log-jottings as I neared the Horn:

December 15th (59th day at sea) Going to head for Cabo Blanco, but this will depend on the wind. I'd like to get a visual check to confirm my position – I haven't seen land since Madeira. I must prepare all my emergency equipment, and consolidate it in one place, just in case. I've got to check all the pumps, and generally make sure that all is in order for a dangerous landfall. One thing to be in deep sea, another to be close to land. There's the danger – land.

December 16th Very little wind. Course 215° (mag). Headed for Cabo Blanco. The barometer has fallen steadily – 'Long foretold, long last'. There's a lot of cirrus about. I think we're in for a wee blow.

December 17th All over the place – the wind has changed nine times today so far! How the hell you keep an accurate DR [dead reckoning] position, I don't know. I look at all the courses, and make a guess. As long as there is plenty of sea, no problem. You get an accurate position from your sights. Listened to Falklands Radio, first to Paul Temple, then to carols. That's when it gets me – how I long to be with Maureen and Samantha. As long as I don't hear anything sad, or carols or such like, I'm OK. I've prepared my emergency equipment and grouped it all. Also stuck instructions on the hanging locker, telling me exactly what to do, so there will be nothing forgotten or mistaken.

December 18th Contacted RMS *Darwin* and spoke to the radio operator, Julian Randell. He gave me further details of the Le Maire Strait, which I'd requested from Captain Miller, master of the *Darwin*. Picked up Port Stanley (Falklands) but they couldn't get me, so a weather bulletin was relayed through Julian. Had a long chat – pleasant to talk to someone again instead of just radioing and reporting. Heard them mention my progress on Falklands Radio tonight. Also they have a photograph on display at the 'Securite', wherever that is.

December 19th My great problem now is whether to make a try to go through the Le Maire Strait, or to go round Staten Island. It's such a dangerous strait. I'll have to make up my mind tomorrow.

December 20th Listening to Falklands Radio, and people from the UK sending their Christmas wishes. I feel so selfish, and absolutely miserable. I try not to think about Christmas at home. It's going to be sad for Maureen and Samantha. I'll be home for every one after this – but that's the trouble with pain, you never remember it.

I reckoned that I should see land on December 21st. I was on edge over the dilemma of whether or not to attempt the Le Maire Strait. It would save what seemed to me then an immense amount of time – but it was a dangerous strait, and I was singlehanded. That was my main worry. The moment I closed land I should have to stay awake – add that to the normal workload on board, and I'd be very tired by the time I got through, and not at all ready to meet the Southern Ocean rolling in from the Pacific. I could make no contact with either Port Stanley or *Darwin* – I heard them calling me, but they couldn't hear me when I answered. It was probably because of the hills.

The decision to go through the Le Maire Strait or round Staten Island was taken from me. The wind being from the south was adverse and I had no option but to go round Staten Island to enter the Pacific.

CHAPTER FOUR

In High Southern Latitudes

On the morning of Monday, December 21st, 1970, I saw land, as I had expected, but after about three quarters of an hour it disappeared in cloud. It was the high ground of Staten Island, about twenty miles away. The wind was a strong northerly, about Force 6, but I picked up a weather forecast from Port Stanley, which suggested that it was going to swing to the south-west. That justified my decision to go round Staten Island, though I hated turning east again. I was worried, too, about clearing the eastern end of Staten Island, and decided to give it a very wide berth.

There were cross-seas all over the place, and I longed to get away from the area and to have sea room again. The barometer was falling, and I didn't like the look of anything. I got no sleep that night and just after lunchtime next day – at 13.10 hours local time – I turned right for the long haul. I was met by a Force 7 wind from the west, with gusts of 40 knots. I was bothered, too, by a number of whales, at least half a dozen of them, which followed me and played around the boat, swimming underneath and surfacing not much more than thirty feet away from me. I had some depth charges ready to try to frighten them off if they seemed likely to hit the boat, but I couldn't help wondering, if I did have to use a depth charge, whether it might simply aggravate them, and make them want to attack me. Fortunately I didn't have to use any explosives, for the whales went away without doing any harm.

Soon after the departure of the whales the wind fell away and the sea became almost calm. I was headed directly for Cape Horn, but without wind I couldn't make much progress. After a lot of difficulty I made contact with Buenos Aires Radio, and received six telegrams of good wishes. These sent me over the moon with delight, for in the loneliness of those seas it was easy to feel that everybody had forgotten me (though I knew quite well they hadn't). I opened my Cape Horn parcel, and inside were a tin of pâté, a tin of potatoes, a tin of mandarin oranges (Maureen's favourite), a game of puzzles and a cake from Eric Lee, my friend at the Admiralty Research Station who had given me so much useful advice on survival. The cake had been made by his wife, and with it was a little note, saying 'Something nice to eat'. Eric was right – I'd eaten almost half the cake before I read the note!

I spent the rest of that day and night at the tiller, edging west. On the morning of December 23rd I was eighty-seven miles from Cape Horn. I'd made radio contact with HMS *Endurance*, which was in the area looking out for me, and we met at 55° 49′S 64° 35′W. (In readiness for our meeting I'd shaved and put on a clean shirt.) I'd given my position as 55° 54′S 64° 44′W, which was about seven miles out. I felt that that was not too bad after sailing over 8,000 miles and without a position line.

Endurance (Captain Rodney Bowden) circled me a couple of times, and two helicopters went up to have a look at me. Then a boat came alongside, manned by Lieutenant Wilkinson, Leading Seamen Virgo, Dennis and Lane, and Leading Airman Dunning. They could be alongside for only a few minutes, but it was great to talk to them. I gave them my mail bags and films, and they gave me a bag with some fresh bread, fruit, and two bottles of whisky. They also gave me a plaque from HMS *Endurance*. Then they went away and it was all over.

I just can't put into words how exciting all this was for me. That meeting, so close to Cape Horn, will remain always one of the highlights of my life. It wasn't luck – not in the least. It was a situation that could have come about only because God willed it. I felt close to God, and very humble.

My log for December 24th (Christmas Eve), 1970, records:

Rounded Horn.

Well, I got round. I went 5 miles to the south of it. Far too close, because of the currents, and also the weather here gets up so quickly. However, I had the opportunity, so I took it. I actually passed it at 19.50 GMT.

I got up this morning after 2 hours' sleep, and there she was, straight on the bow. When I got close I felt the loneliness of the place. When I passed it I had a wee toast with wine, and said 'Goody – Atlantic – Pacific.'

It was calm for about an hour. Had contact with the Falklands. Problem is, I'm so tired. I've had about 4 hours' sleep in the last three days, trying to get the best out of her.

Now I'm SW of the Horn, and the wind is from the SW. This causes a problem because I can't get too far north. I don't want to get boxed in. Must keep sea room. I've got those bloody islands [the Cape Horn archipelago] to worry about, and they are unlighted. Ah well, we'll get by, but it's going to be a fight all the way.

The seas are certainly changing. They are looking much more formidable. Not to worry. Can't last for ever (or can it?).

Christmas Eve in UK now, all the Santas filling the stockings. I feel very sad, and somehow deprived of something.

Had my Cape Horn meal – crab, tin of ham, roast potatoes, glass of wine. Far too early for champagne, and I've got to keep alert, so no whisky or spirits.

The cabin was horribly untidy, and dirty dishes from the past three days' meals were still unwashed. This was visible evidence of my tiredness. Partly by nature and partly because of my Army training I am a fairly tidy person, and I hated the cabin's being in such a mess. But I was just too exhausted to do anything about it.

On Christmas Day the weather worsened, with the wind a full gale – Force 8 – gusting to Force 9. The seas were enormous, with a quality of sheer bigness that was new and menacing. My Christmas present from the Southern Ocean was a disaster – a huge sea hit the yacht and smashed the self-steering gear beyond repair. I was hurled across the cockpit, my head hit the door of the companion way and my forehead was gashed open. It was a deep, nasty cut, but I was far more concerned about the self-steering gear. With that out of action the whole voyage had to be seen in a different light. It was going to take far longer than I'd calculated. Unless I stayed at the tiller I couldn't get close to the wind, and I couldn't stay at the tiller all the time. To get rest I'd often have to heave-to, getting nowhere, or even dropping backwards and losing some of the miles that I'd so painfully gained. I felt absolutely shattered. Then I heard my own name on the Merchant Navy Programme – they were playing 'Moon River' requested for me by Maureen and Samantha. That somehow put fresh heart into me. I determined that the sea should not have me, that I was going to get home to my wife and daughter. Just how, or how long it might take, did not then bother me: I was simply determined to do it.

The gale blew all night and eventually I hove-to because I feared for the sails. I couldn't eat anything; all I could do was to curl up in my sleeping bags and try to keep some warmth in my body.

Boxing Day brought little change in the weather, though the wind moderated a little to around Force 7. The wind was still in the north-west and I was being forced south. I didn't want to go too far south because of the danger of ice – every mile south increased the danger of icebergs. I failed to make radio contact with Port Stanley and this bothered me, because if I couldn't get through with a radio message I feared that people would start worrying about me.

British Steel was sailing well, and riding the huge seas gallantly. But every now and then a wave would hit her and stop her almost dead. I couldn't steer by hand for long at a time because it was so desperately cold; also I felt that clinging to the tiller was bad for my morale. I'd lost the self-steering gear, yes, but it was my job to fix up something to keep going. I could lash the tiller, but with the tiller lashed I couldn't get the yacht to do better than 60° to the wind, and even then it was hard for her to hold a course with great seas stopping her all the time. I doubt if I have ever felt more miserable in my life. I felt sick, not with seasickness but with worry. I'd opened my Christmas presents on Christmas Eve. My friends really did me proud with cards and gifts but instead of cheering me up they made me want to cry. Now I packed them all away again except for two decorations and Eric Lee's calendar with photographs of Scotland. I decided to open all my presents again later, when the weather was better.

On December 27th the sun came out for a bit and the wind went round to the south-east. It also moderated, though it was soon blowing about Force 6 again – Force 5, 6 and 7 seem to be the normal winds in that part of the world. I took advantage of the sun to have a bath and a shave but even then I had to use the shelter of the doghouse because of the wind-chill factor. I also washed some socks. The bandage

I'd put round the cut in my head was caked with salt, but I thought it would do for another day before I changed it. I managed to get through on the radio, and sent a message telling of the mishap to the self-steering gear. I heard on the radio of the death of Lillian Board, and this made me feel very sad.

My log records how my mood changed with each little incident of the voyage.

December 28th 57° 10′S 78° 10′W. Pleasant surprise when I worked out my position – didn't think I was that far west. Navigation really isn't a problem just now. It's a waste of time bothering too much – I don't worry as long as I'm going basically west.

Contacted Port Stanley. Received cable from Maureen and Phil, obviously worried as to what I'm going to do. Well, that's easy – keep going as long as I can.

Heard of two tankers crippled in the Atlantic. I prayed all will be saved. The sea is a miserable place to die.

I'm now on the Pacific chart. You have South America on the extreme right, then nothing. I've folded it in half so that I don't see all the sea. This way I don't think it's so far; completely nutty, but it helps.

Great Alby [albatross] has been following me for about two days now. Goodness knows what size he is, but he's the biggest I've seen so far. He has a white belly with brown wings, with two white spots on his wings, one on each. He's the only one that will swoop down to examine a biscuit. Don't know if he eats it, but at least he has a look.

Thinking about my return, and where I'll take Maureen and Samantha for a week's holiday.

December 29th I'm in one hell of a turmoil. The wind's from the west. Do I go on 210° (Mag) which gives me 232° (True), or 340° (Mag), which gives me 2° (True)?

With 232° (True) I get westing, but also southing. I fear for the metal; with this cold the metal becomes very much more brittle. I'm also well into the ice area. Or do I go north and slightly east – lose westing, but gain northing? I've become obsessed with westing. At present I'm on the 232° (True).

I pray for guidance and that the wind should swing to the SW. It will swing to the SW, but the problem is when.

No contact with Port Stanley – overslept.

Well, I prayed for northing and now the wind's shifted to 260° (Mag) which gives me 283° (True). That's a wonderful course. How long will it last? What is needed is faith and belief in God.

Favourite dinner tonight, pasties. They really are great. I have a sherry before each evening meal.

December 30th Barometer's steadily dropping. I feel terrible. The yacht's heeled over, it's very cold and all I want to do is stay in my sleeping bag. To add to my discomfort I'm sleeping in the windward bunk because of leaks. Got some northing, but not much – 30 miles.

Stores are beginning to show signs of continual using. The first thing I will run out of is tea bags. Pity, I enjoy a good cup of tea, and this is good tea. It isn't because Maureen underestimated, it's because I didn't allow enough for the wind chill. The result is that I'm drinking far more than I would be if I was running before the wind.

Great fear here is equipment. It's all beginning to show signs of wear. With the continual bashing I've become a little punch-drunk. I find it really is an effort to do anything. This is one reason why I want to get north. It won't be so bad if it's a little warmer.

I had thought, indeed everyone I consulted had predicted, that in these high southern latitudes I should make great long tacks, staying on one tack for days at a time. So far my tacks had all proved to be short ones, of fifty to seventy miles. The wind changed all the time, not often great changes, but always changes. It was never, never steady. The cold was worse than I'd expected, and I couldn't get my heating stove to go at all. I stripped it down and tried hard to find out what was wrong, but nothing I could do made much difference and in the end I gave it up and did without it.

Apart from the bash on my head, I was physically in pretty good shape. My hands were sore and forming callouses, especially my right hand between the thumb and the first finger. This is where the rope slips through when dropping the sails. I kept up my programme of exercises as well as I could. It took a real mental effort to do them, but I always felt the better for it. Particularly when beating, I had a job to keep my feet warm. The hard part about beating as opposed to running is that every time you go on the foredeck you get soaked. The bow is continually crashing into waves, and spray pours on board. Sometimes I wore my skin diving boots, and found them quite efficient in helping to keep warmth in my feet. I washed my socks whenever I could, though it was often hard to get them dry. I found that putting on clean socks – indeed, clean anything – always seemed to raise my spirits. So did a wash and shave. Cooking was often hard work – balancing yourself over the galley stove in a wildly kicking boat is no joke. But hot food is vital to morale, and even when I felt that the galley stove was the last thing I ever wanted to see again, self-discipline and Para training came to the rescue, and there were few days when I didn't have at least one proper meal.

On Auld Year's Day I opened my New Year's Day pack. It contained a Scottish calendar, and my flag as first Commodore of the Antarctic Yacht Club. This was made up by Anne Ingram and her children. I decided to fly it from the spreaders when I got home, and I thought – that will confuse them! My pack also had a tin of chicken, crab and other goodies. My heart went out to Maureen for the infinite trouble she had gone to in preparing these little treats for me.

I got a pleasant surprise when I took a couple of sights. I'd reported my position to Port Stanley as 57° 20′S and 84° 40′W. I now found that I was 56° 08′S, 87°W, a lot farther both north and west than I'd estimated. I was delighted. I thought that perhaps there was a current helping me north.

I had two New Year celebrations, one by GMT, one by local time. GMT was some seven hours ahead of me, and as it neared midnight GMT I thought of all that would be happening at home. There would be a party at the club, and in Scotland – especially in Hawick – the wives would have their houses spick and span, with the currant bun cut, and biscuits, and the bottle waiting for the men, who would just be leaving the pub to wait on their first foot ('fit' in Scotland!). Well, I sang 'Auld Lang Syne' all the way through, and I toasted Maureen, Samantha and family, Frank and Audrey and all my friends, with the words 'To all I say Good Cheer and God Bless You'.

For my own New Year party I had a dinner of chicken, butter beans and peas, with a glass of wine. I gave myself a sherry before dinner, and at twelve o'clock I opened my bottle of whisky and had a wee dram. Then bed. Outside it was blowing westerly at about 10 knots and *British Steel* was only doing 4 knots. It seemed a reasonably gentle night, and as I turned in I gave myself another treat: I decided to sleep the night through.

New Year's Day, 1971, brought the best day's sail I'd had since the self-steering gear went. It put me well to the north, and was marred only by a rogue wave hitting me and half-filling the cockpit. It also came in through the cabin door.

As I got north it got a little warmer. I finished reading *Seal Morning* and thoroughly enjoyed it, and I started writing letters to be handed over at my next rendezvous off Tasmania. There was a lot of cirrus about, but the barometer was steady. I had an enormous meal of steak and kidney pie with pastry, butter beans, peas, onions and roast potatoes. It really was enormous, and I enjoyed every mouthful.

I was getting out of radio range of Port Stanley. On January 2nd I made contact, heard him say 'I've a message for you', and then no more. But I had fantastic luck with Wellington, New Zealand. I'd had a message saying that Wellington would be listening for me between 12.00 and 15.00 GMT. At 13.00 I tuned in and heard their call, but never for a moment did I expect to make contact at this distance. But I had a go, and back came the answer, 'ZLW answering *British Steel*. You are strength 3.' I was overjoyed, like a boy with a new toy. I sent a telegram to the British Steel Corporation saying that I was in contact with New Zealand, and arranged a weekly schedule. It was great to hear them, and I had a lovely chat with the operator. He said that the temperature was 76° in Wellington. I felt that I couldn't get north fast enough!

Then it started to blow again, but the wind was from the south-west, and I could make a grand course of 316° (True). It went up to Force 9, and I thought that I really ought to heave-to or lie a-hull, but *British Steel* was going so well under No 3 boomed foresail and reefed mizzen that I hated to stop her. I decided that if the wind didn't moderate soon I'd have to lie a-hull: to go on would be taking too great a risk of breaking something. I was bothered because the night before the galley drawer came adrift and everything crashed to the floor, knives, the lot – *and I didn't even hear it*! I feared that if I hadn't heard that I might not hear anything on deck.

In the middle of the night the wind went up to Force 10

and I went on deck and dropped the No 3 jib and reefed mizzen. I left my little foresail jib up and the tiller lashed down. The little sail helped to steady her. With everything checked I went back to bed but I got up at daybreak to go outside and see what was happening. She looked all right. We were making some heading at about 3 knots, but as it was north I didn't mind. The wind, however, increased still more, gusting to Force 11, and I lay a-hull for about five hours. Then the wind moderated to about Force 8, and I couldn't bear to wait any longer, so got under way. I felt quite safe inside the hull; what I feared was the equipment breaking up. But it didn't, though how the gear and the hull stood the battering they got in that storm I don't know. I found lying a-hull – that is, simply leaving your boat, under bare masts, to behave like a cork and not resist the sea in any way – very frustrating. It was like being becalmed, except that you had fear to contend with as well.

The storm blew itself out after two days, but I got a shock when I took my noon sight on January 6th. I estimated that I had been blown about 100 miles north – it turned out to be 200 miles. That shows you the sort of storm it was. I suspected my sight and checked it, but it seemed to be OK.

I made radio contact with the Falklands and also with New Zealand, where I spoke to an operator called Roger White. It seems that radio operators all round the world are nice and helpful. I was saying goodbye to the Falklands. The operators there had been very good to me, and I was sorry that we shouldn't be calling each other any more. But to be out of range of the Falklands meant that I was getting on, and that was what I wanted.

A strange thing happened on the morning of January 7th. I got up with an overpowering feeling that something had happened to Samantha So strong was this feeling that I stopped what I was doing to say a special prayer for Samantha and Maureen. When I got home I learned that Samntha had knocked out one of her front teeth a few days before. It is possible that when I had that feeling that something had happened to her, her mouth was hurting her. She, of course, has long forgotten just what occurred to her on January 7th. I'm sure that in some strange way we were suddenly in mental or spiritual contact with each other.

My own teeth were all right, but I began having trouble with my ears, which came out in a rash and itched horribly. I treated them with some cream, and the trouble gradually cleared up.

I became obsessed with passing 100°W. I thought of each 10° space on the chart as a 'barrier', and was always delighted when I crossed one. This particular 10° seemed the most barrier-like of all, and I longed to overcome it. I managed this on January 8th, and celebrated by folding the chart to get rid of South America. I seemed to have been in the South American area for ever, and it was a joy to feel that at last I was beyond it.

The bit of ocean I was now in was marked on the weather chart as being subject to fog. Sure enough I met fog, and it was really thick. It was eerie to be crashing along at 7–8 knots in thick fog, somehow more eerie than sailing in fog in the Channel or the Atlantic. But really it was much less dangerous. In my lonely latitudes to hit another ship would have been a chance of many millions to one. That fog lasted for four days. My log tells how I occupied myself.

January 9th Third day of fog. Don't know why, but I feel depressed and homesick – I long to see Maureen and Samantha. I tried to take my mind off thinking of them both by cleaning the galley and the cooker. I now have a sparkling clean galley and cooker. Reading *The Centurion*, about the French Paras. Reminds me of the days of great comradeship, when I was a Para. Those were wonderful days fit, arrogant, and a great feeling of

well-being. Slowly it all went sour. I'd like to see and have
a drink with some of the paratroopers again, but I suppose to do so would be an anticlimax. But they were
wonderful days.

January 10th Fourth day of fog. It's been a miserable
day, with rain and fog all the time. Visibility is down to
about 20 yards. I collected about 6 gallons of water. I
could have got a lot more, but there's no point. I've a
whole tank full yet. The sun did break through for about
an hour. I took the opportunity to have a haircut. My hair
was quite long, and it was driving me batty. Now it's
short. I washed it and myself all over, and also had a
shave. Feel a lot better. Clean clothes – I even changed my
pillowcase and trousers.

The fog lifted next day – to be followed by a calm that
was, if anything, more miserable than fog. Even in a calm
there was still an enormous swell, built up by the gales that
have swept these high southern latitudes from the beginning
of time. With no wind to hold her *British Steel* rolled like a
drunkard. It's hard to explain how frustrating I found this
period of the voyage. I found myself cursing the whole place
violently, and then I was ashamed of behaving so childishly.
So I embarked on a no-swearing campaign, devising various
small punishments for myself if I broke the rules.

To add to the misery of that frustrating calm, my feet
began to hurt abominably with chilblains. At times they
were quite excruciatingly painful – I wouldn't have believed
it possible that chilblains could hurt so much.

After tacking at least fifteen miles to try to make the most
of whatever zephyr of wind there was I gave up, dropped all
the sails and went to bed in the middle of the afternoon.

In the small hours next morning the wind came back, and
we crashed along north-west at 7–8 knots. I now had a bit of
a problem. I'd worked out a DR position which put me

where I thought I was, but a sight – not a good one – disagreed. I was either farther north than I'd reckoned, or the current was stronger than I'd allowed for. I remembered how far out I'd been in reckoning my northing during the storm and began to wonder if some new deviation had crept into my compass: I thought it possible that with all the bashing we had had the magnetic fields in the hull might have moved. I determined to check the compass on the first decent day. Meanwhile I accepted the position that my sight gave me instead of my own dead-reckoning. Thinking it over, I began to see where I had probably gone wrong. For much of the time I'd been sheeted in hard, and sailing as close to the wind as I could. With the self-steering gear out of action the yacht often yawed violently. I'd been taking an estimated mean between yaws as the average course, but this must have been fairly inaccurate, and not allowed enough for the times when we'd been simply moving with the wind. This didn't rule out a possible error in the compass as well – I thought that probably there was an error, perhaps around 10°.

My sight put me at 46° 04′S. I didn't really want to go farther north than 45°S at this stage of the voyage, so I'd only a degree or so of northing in hand. But there wasn't very much I could do about it – I had to go where the wind took me.

I had a sudden longing to be back in Hawick, taking Samantha and Maureen round the wonderful park there. I wanted to get off the boat and *run* round the park. I remembered how Maureen and I had played on the putting green there. Actually, I didn't much like playing with Maureen, because she always beat me! I reflected that I could always play with Samantha – surely I could beat her! (On further reflection, I was not so sure!)

On January 14th, my eighty-ninth day at sea, I finished my first bottle of gas for the galley stove. It had lasted well,

and as I changed the bottles I concluded that I should hav
plenty of gas to see the voyage through. It poured with rai
for most of the day, but I didn't bother to collect any be
cause I had ample fresh water on board. I had one rathe
startling experience when I thought for a moment that I'
seen a ghost. A queer cloud of white vapour suddenly ap
peared from nowhere about 400 feet away. Then I saw tha
it was a big whale spouting, and that the cloud was forme
by the spray left when he spouted. I was startled in
different way by a book I was reading called *Dare to b
Free*. The author said that he was in a 14-foot boat whic
did 12 knots! I wished I had him with me!

The wind fell light again and on January 15th my day
run was only thirty-eight miles. I'd gone still farther nortl
to 44° 45'S, and I began to try to make a bit of southing fo
a change. I was in a barometric 'high' which was giving m
these light airs, and I wanted to get out of it. Without wind
could do nothing. Any sort of wind then seemed better tha
a calm.

I got my wish next day, with a westerly gusting to Force
I spent a long time on deck trying to get *British Steel* to ste
herself. This was slow work. For what seemed ages
couldn't understand why she just wouldn't go, but gradual
I was able to work out things and eventually I got it. I we
below feeling frozen to the bone. This is the sort of tin
when a singlehander really misses a crew – there was r
mate below to hand me a nice hot cup of coffee. I stoo
myself a gin and tonic, and it tasted wonderful. I'm not at a
sure that it isn't just the tonic that I liked drinking, though
admit that the gin does give it a wee bit extra.

I did a particularly silly thing on January 17th. I went o
deck before breakfast, and found myself beginning to shak
I knew the feeling quite well – it was a sure sign that
needed something to eat. When I was in the Army I alwa
took one Mars bar for every day that I expected to be awa

The departure: Chay on his own at last. The escort boats
turned back before the Needles

British Steel was launched on August 19th, 1970, only four months after the first steel had been cut for the hull

The cabin, looking forward

Chay and Winston, his lion mascot, made of rope. Winston is on his second world trip. He sailed first with Sir Alec Rose who gave him to Chay

Mending the mainsail

The waves that accompanied *British Steel* by day . . .

. . . and by night

'There she is' – Chay sights the Horn

Checking the self-steering gear

Necessary repairs to the running sail booms

Below deck Chay works out a sight

A triumphant return

Maureen, Chay and Samantha – together again, at home

British Steel

an exercise; if the feeling came over me, all I did was to
eat a Mars bar, and then I was OK. This morning I ignored
the feeling, and kept working on deck. It was a stupid thing
to do, especially as I had on board a big box of Mars bars,
which Maureen had packed for just such occasions. After
about an hour and a half on deck I felt as weak as a kitten.
Then I did pack in, went below and had a huge breakfast of
four eggs, three sausages, three cups of tea and about a
dozen cream crackers with marmalade. That restored me all
right, but I was still cross with myself: what would have
happened if some emergency had cropped up when I was
feeling faint through my own fault for just not eating? I
determined that it must never happen again.

Deck leaks were a constant irritation as I moved on across
the vast spaces of the Pacific. The best of boats is always
liable to let in water somewhere in the cabin, and it is often
extraordinarily difficult to discover precisely where it is
coming from. With all the battering we had had I could
scarcely blame *British Steel* for letting in some sea here and
there, but these leaks were a great nuisance, and I spent
hours trying to trace them. A particularly irritating leak
was over one of the bunks, which meant that unless I
could stop it the bunk was unusable because my sleeping
bag just got soaked. It is much more comfortable to sleep on
a lee berth – here is an advantage of sailing singlehanded, for
you can change bunks as you like. With the leak, I couldn't;
and it was no fun having to wedge myself in to try to sleep to
windward. At last I thought that I had really fixed the leak,
and I looked forward to a comfortable night in the lee berth.
But no joy – the leak was almost as bad as ever, and when I
got up my sleeping bag was sopping. It took a whole day to
dry it out with the hot-water bottle.

This was a lonely part of the world, and the sea didn't
seem to have much life; at least, not much visible life, for no
doubt the waters were really teeming with life of all sorts. I

saw one enormous fish, about twelve feet long, which l
out of the water like a young salmon and consid
startled me. And there were occasional dolphins,
always gave me great pleasure. Down below, I could lis
them through the hull, and hear them frolicking abou
sure I heard one squeal. He must have been directly
the hull when we left the top of a wave and crashed
and either we hit him or we gave him a terrible frigh
certain he let out a squeal. I hoped he wasn't hurt.

I continued to do rather silly little things from ti
time. One was to eat a whole packet of dates straight
didn't feel so hot afterwards, and added eating-too-n
dates to my list of resolutions of things not to do.

On Monday evening, January 18th, I heard over the
that a postal strike was threatened in the UK for th
lowing Wednesday (January 20th). Thursday wasn't n
for calling Wellington, but I decided to try to call th
get a message through to Phil Wolfinden before the
started. Just as I tuned in for Wellington I heard them
me! They said they had a telegram for me, but it wa
good contact so I said I'd wait and have a go next day
I was due for a scheduled call. I did manage to put
short telegram to Phil giving him my position, and I
he'd get that at any rate even if the strike did interfer
telegrams.

That was another long day of rain and fog, with
nating calms and squalls. In the space of ninety mir
had wind blowing at Force 5 from the west, then calm
wind from the north, calm again, then Force 5 fro
south! It was certainly a weird part of the ocean, and
calms, squalls and wind changes made for endless w
sail changing and jockeying with the tiller lines to g
best out of the yacht. I made another determined ef
locate the leaks over my bunk, and got nowhere. I was
I was stuck with them – unless *British Steel* correcte

erself. Doghouse and deck leaks on boats are mysterious things; they come mysteriously, and sometimes (though, alas, not very often) just as mysteriously they go away. I decided to give myself a Scottish dinner, a kind of dress rehearsal for Burns Night. I had haggis, roast potatoes, and peas, and with the haggis I had a dram of whisky. Man, it was good stuff! It really did enhance the haggis.

The miserable weather went on for several days. The wind was all over the place, but it had a spell in the north-east and ran with the main and mizzen goose-winged. I had to adjust the tiller continually, though, and as it was pouring with rain I sat under a space blanket to try to keep warm. In the end I went below and led tiller lines to the cabin. It was like being on a horse with long reins, but it was better than being outside, and I could leave her for a few minutes at a time – just long enough to get a meal. In spite of having to leap back and forth from the galley to the tiller lines, I was pleased with the yacht's performance, and reckoned that with a suitable wind she would run all right with the main and mizzen out.

Nothing lasted long, and as soon as I'd got her settled goose-winged the wind swung round to the north-west and I was close-hauled. That's how it went on. The rain went on, too, and I collected about six gallons to do some washing. I also washed my hair. Some log-notes from this period:

January 20th Contacted NZ and they are sending my reports by Telex due to the postal strike. Asked if I would officially open the Birmingham Boat Show. What a surprise! I was delighted – pity I'll miss it. The last time I saw the sun was five days ago. All the time the DR error gets greater. Still, as long as I'm moving on, not back. Can't keep accurate DR with all this yawing. Course indicator is sticking. That means no off-course alarm. That's a blow.

January 21st What a day's sail! Up and down – it's gone from Force 2 to Force 7 all day. Rain and fog. It's poured like the monsoon. Everywhere down below is soaked, there are wet clothes hanging everywhere. The leaks over the bunk are a continuous stream. I had a good breakfast – mushrooms and eggs. I really enjoyed them. An enormous curry for dinner. I was up twice last night and I've been outside almost continually all day. I'm shattered. To get away from the fog I think I'll have to go north or south.

January 22nd Fog. Calm all last night but at 04.30 it got up to Force 3. So away we went, but it wasn't much. At 09.30 it was Force 1, then went calm. Took the opportunity of having a wash all over and a shave. I didn't need a shave, but it's always nice to have one. Had a couple of hours' sleep and at 16.30 I awoke to see the start of a storm. Wind went straight to Force 7, then Force 8 gusting 9. I hope to goodness I don't have to go on deck. I can see the waves from the porthole sweeping straight across the deck. Thank goodness Robert [Clark] made it flush. Heard Radio Peking, so I sang them 'The Road and Miles to Dundee' – as an imperialist marching song! Don't think they liked it!

January 23rd Astro position 45° 30′S, 134° 50′W. Pleasant surprise to get my position. First time I've seen the sun for 8 days. Didn't think I was so far west.

First lot of food finished – my crisps. They lasted well.

Taking a sight and a whale came up right alongside, not 5 ft away. What a fright – I cursed him. He just ignored me and pushed off.

Discovered a Christmas parcel containing a Scottish calendar and Christmas cards from members of the Club. It really cheered me up.

Wind Force 1. Took the opportunity of doing some

maintenace. 1. Painted compass box 2. Seized main and whipped foresail halyard 3. Patched main 4. Dried clothing and sleeping bags 5. Tightened forestay.

Good dinner – sherry, meat pasty, roast potatoes, celery and wine.

After that dinner I had a wonderful sleep, and didn't get up until 09.00. It was about the best night's sleep I'd had on the voyage; and not only that, but my sleeping bag was dry (thanks to yesterday's sun) and not damp, as it usually was. My fine night's sleep was a good thing, for I couldn't get the yacht to steer herself and sat at the tiller for eleven continuous hours. I passed the time by making jokes to myself, and drawing up imaginary telegrams to send to people. I thought of sending the Commodore of the Sailing Club this one – 'Thought of a good one to replace Hamble Scramble. Leave Sydney to starboard and guess the course.' Alas, the only people who would appreciate that would be those who know our Hamble Scramble!

January 25th was my hundredth day at sea. It was calm and the only point of interest was that I saw my first shark. I put in another long stint at the tiller and sang thirty-eight songs. I was surprised to find that I knew so many.

It was frustrating sailing. I had only 4° of longitude to cross to get off the eastern sheet of the chart of the Southern Ocean. I longed to get off that chart sheet and on to the next, and I could have done it in about twenty-four hours – with wind! But there wasn't any decent wind; it was either calm or blowing like hell from the wrong direction. I consulted my log and counted up and I found that since rounding the Horn I'd had 149 hours of non-sailing, either from calms or from lying a-hull in bad weather.

It took me two more days to get off that chart-sheet but the great moment came and I marked in my position on the western sheet – *which showed New Zealand*! I sat for a few minutes almost hypnotized. I thought, 'One day I'll get past New Zealand!' And I reflected, 'That will be something. Yes, that will be an achievement as far as I am concerned. It's been hard.'

I came out of my reverie and celebrated by opening a tin of prawns. I had only twelve tins on board, and this was the first I'd opened. I also opened my last tin of mushrooms. Lord, but they were nice!

I was still unhappy about my compass. I took an amplitude. I made it 10°E deviation, but I wasn't all that sure of it. Being hard on the wind for so much of the time, and without self-steering gear, I had to put up with a good deal of variation in course. I decided to make every check I could from day to day.

But I was getting on. On January 28th I entered yet another time-zone, and I was getting near the International Date Line. I began to think of trade winds, and the flying fish and the sun. I saw myself choking down a Pepsi and saying, 'It's hell in this hot sun.' I'd almost forgotten what it was like. I told myself, 'One day, yes, one day you'll be homeward bound, to Maureen and Samantha.'

On January 29th I opened my Burns Pack. I had always thought that Burns Night was January 25th, but Maureen had put down the 29th and I supposed that she was right (she usually is). But this time she was wrong, for Burns Night *is* the 25th. However, it worked out well enough, for it gave me my haggis dinner in rather better weather.

My Burns Pack contained a haggis, plus all the other ingredients, and a menu card for a Burns Dinner. There was an additional nice surprise in a book *The Survival of Scotland*, from the Bath and District Caledonian Society, presented by Dr J. M. Samson. I was delighted with it. That was a good day for surprises. I found a jar of honey that I didn't know I had, and a St Christopher medal in one of the locker drawers.

Perhaps the little St Christopher brought me luck, for
ext day I was able to confirm my suspicions about the
ompass. There was a good and clearly visible sunset, and
aat gave me a good check. I had no azimuth ring for the
ompass, but I improvised with a ruler to line up on. It was
ot a hundred per cent perfect, but a lot better than nothing.
Iy check confirmed the 10°E deviation that I had sus-
ected, and knowing where I stood with the compass made
ae a lot happier. I opened my only tin of shortcake to cele-
rate.

I was now at 44° 05′S, and this was further north than I
anted to be to edge past New Zealand. I reckoned that I
eeded to go some 300 miles farther south. I should have
ked to have kept more southing, but I couldn't control the
inds. Now I had to make that southing, and I set a course
aat would give it to me. I was able to hold it through most
f January 31st, but the first day of February brought
nother calm, and I stayed more or less in the same place for
bout sixteen hours. It was a drag, but I managed to get
ome useful maintenance done, painted the forehatch and
enerally tidied up. I also stitched the mizzen. One of the
attens was almost out, and the sail torn. I planed the batten
own a bit and repaired the sail. On this day I saw my first
ign of land since leaving Cape Horn – a lot of kelp floating
bout. There isn't much land in this part of the ocean, but
aere are a few small islands to the east and south-east of
lew Zealand – Bounty Island, Antipodes Island and Camp-
ell Island. The kelp may have come from one of these – I
ook it as a sure sign that land could not be very far away.
'wo days later (February 3rd) I saw a lot of birds, another
ood sign that land still existed in the world.

I had still a good way to go to reach New Zealand, but I
ad to consider my course carefully. It would never do to be
riven too far north, but I found it hard work trying to
et south. I could have gone south-east without much

difficulty, but that would mean going backwards! And this simply couldn't contemplate. Well, I'd set out to sail round the world against the prevailing winds, a voyage that som people said would be impossible for a singlehander. I'd come nearly halfway round the world. It was just a question of battling on.

I was having difficulty in making radio contact as I neared New Zealand – radio conditions are often easier over long distances than relatively short ones. I was bothered tha Maureen might be worried at hearing nothing of me, par ticularly so because my radio had been on the whole so good since leaving the Horn. Again, I could but go on trying. If couldn't get Wellington, I might soon be able to raise Chat ham Island. Sometimes I could hear Wellington calling me but they couldn't hear me.

Gales continued to alternate with calms, coming suddenly and causing all sorts of upsets. One was to try to take away my dinner. I'd laid on the chart table, turned to get th salt, and the next moment most of the dinner was on th chart table. I just put it all back on the plate and ate it Mercifully, I'd made it a habit to put away charts and book as I finished using them, so the dinner didn't do any damage Another time a rogue wave filled the cockpit and splashe through the door onto my sleeping bag. I tried to dry the ba with a hot-water bottle – but try filling a hot-water bottle i a gale! I reckoned that only about one-fifth of my hot wate went in.

Sometimes I'd get a nice sunset, with 'red sky at night' But 'red sky at night' meant absolutely nothing in these lati tudes. It might bring a good day; it might equally well brin an absolutely awful one.

CHAPTER FIVE

New Zealand and Tasmania

The Southern Ocean seemed to go on for ever. I thought of other small-boat voyages in the Pacific – none had ever been my way. Joshua Slocum, the father of singlehanded sailing, had gone round the world from east to west, but after sailing through the Magellan Strait he had gone north, to the kindly, warm Pacific, with its delectable string of South Sea islands. Chichester, Rose, and Knox-Johnston, my recent predecessors in singlehanded circumnavigations, had gone south into the Roaring Forties, but they all sailed the other way. The Forties, in a sense, roared *with* them. I had deliberately challenged the Forties to roar *against* me. I couldn't grumble if my progress across the chart seemed painfully slow. At least it *was* progress, and I could be thankful for a sound and gallant boat, for keeping basically fit in spite of chilblains, ear-rashes and other minor ills, and for all the splendid stores that Maureen and my friends had provided for me.

The lines of longitude that I thought of to myself as barriers across the chart were slowly surmounted and falling behind. I crossed 160°W, and felt enormously elated. Only another 20° and I should have come halfway around the world! I still couldn't bear to think of total distances; I kept myself going by thinking of the voyage as a series of obstacle races – only another 16° to pass Chatham Island, then 5° to pass Bounty Island, and so on. I couldn't accept that I'd still got 180° to cross before my second right turn – at the Cape of Good Hope – and the beginning of the long run home. So I didn't think of it like that, except to feel sure in my heart that somehow and on some day I *would* get there.

When the sky was clear at night I gazed up at the moon, thinking of the brave men who had gone there. Somehow that made my own problems seem utterly insignificant. What was this Force 9 wind that I was worrying about, when men journeyed to the moon? But that was a philosophical rather than a practical reflection. My voyage might be insignificant compared to theirs, but the waves brought by my Force 9 were real, and close at hand. Those waves! They came hissing towards me like snow-capped mountains. Sometimes the cockpit would fill, and *British Steel* and I would seem to be buried under great masses of foaming water. But always she would climb out again. I would just sit in the cabin grinning like a Cheshire cat – not because I wasn't afraid, for I was often afraid, but because that's the way it's always taken me. The worse the situation gets the funnier it seems!

My log records of this period:

February 4th It was still blowing Force 8 at 10.00 and then it started to drop. Incredible how quickly it dropped. It left very confused seas, waves seeming to go in all directions. Continual sail alteration – ie, sheeting in, reefing mizzen and unreefing. No contact with New Zealand – Maureen won't have had a position report now for 2 weeks.

February 5th It has been a rotten day, squalls and gusts all day. One minute 15-knot wind, then 35 knots. All from the SW. Tried to contact Chatham Island, but no go.

February 6th All day it's been up and down with squalls, all day I've done nothing but tack. Now I'm going due south. To hell with it, I'll get west one day. It just seems that the 25° of longitude to pass New Zealand are going to be one hard struggle. Not to worry – one day the Trade Winds. Contacted Chatham Island. They said Wellington had over 300 words of telegrams for me. They couldn't relay to Chatham and they to me, I don't know why. Had a wash and shave and nice clean clothing. Boy, I needed that.

February 7th Severe squalls. I spilt a cup of tea over me, due to taking off from the top of a wave. I'll write of one squall. Great cumulus clouds on the horizon, at present blowing Force 7. As they get closer they get dark and towering; eventually they are black. You watch it, and you see the white forming on the already big sea. Then it comes – the wind up to 55 knots. I have to be on the tiller –anything over 45 knots I take it. Means I'm going NE (ie away from New Zealand). I try to keep running to an absolute minimum. For approximately 5–10 minutes it blows very hard. Now the rain – it's like hailstones, but it isn't. The rain stings my face and hands, gets up my sleeves and makes me all damp in my suit. The first batch of rain goes, and is followed by more rain. Rather like a sandstorm. Then it's gone, and there's no wind, the seas are lumpy, and you just get thrown about and the sails flap. This lasts only 5–10 minutes. Then you are off again, Force 7.

During these squalls I'd sing or shout at *British Steel*, saying, 'Come on *Brit* – flat out! Show me the way home. Maureen and Samantha are waiting.' I would pretend to be whipping on my steed. It may sound silly, written down like this, but without those little games I'd have been utterly miserable. As it was, I was usually quite cheerful in squalls, although I felt the whole performance an awful drag.

In spite of the squalls on February 7th I managed to make

radio contact with Wellington and received their telegrams. I also got one of the new programmes on the radio. It seemed mostly about riots in Ireland. They made me feel terribly sad. On a more domestic note, I was frying some chips and the pan spilt. It happened as we slid down a wave. There was a horrible mess, with oil everywhere.

On February 9th I heard Chatham Island Radio give out a gale warning. I thought it a great joke, for I'd had gales for three days. On this day I crossed the International Date Line, but I didn't change the date at once. It didn't seem to matter when I changed it.

I spent the whole of the next day (February 10th) lying a-hull (Chatham Island's gale, I supposed). The wind, from the south-west, varied between Force 9 and 10. It was nerve-racking, waiting for the big fellows to come at me. I tried to take some photographs and ended up by getting the camera soaked. Then I had an enormous curry and took the chance to catch up on some sleep.

In the usual way that gale was followed by a calm, and I thought I'd have my postponed Burns Night Party. I secured all the sails, and down below I combed my hair, cleaned my teeth, and prepared dinner. I had to do a lot of juggling with pans, for I only had two burners, but eventually I had my party. The haggis was great, washed down with whisky. I drank a quarter of a bottle. I read Burns out loud, sang all the Scottish songs I knew, and toasted all my friends. Then bed – to sleep for twelve hours.

I woke with a splitting headache, which lasted all day. It served me right – but it had been a grand party! And it did me a lot of good, for after all the battering I'd had I think I was probably beginning to suffer from mental fatigue. The psychological release of my party, followed by twelve hours' sleep, seemed to put me on my feet again.

I was now just 500 miles from New Zealand. I saw a marker buoy drift by, and a new kind of bird – sure signs that land was really getting near. I expected that I'd soon start seeing some ships and decided to put on my masthead light at night – I didn't want a collision at that stage!

On February 14th I advanced the date, changing my calendar to recognize my crossing of the International Date Line a few days back. I began to feel really excited. I'd crossed 180° of longitude *west* of Greenwich and was now on longitude *east* of Greenwich. That meant halfway round the world. Now every degree of longitude was one degree nearer home, whereas before it was only one degree nearer to climbing 180°. I opened another tin of prawns to celebrate. I was getting great radio contacts. Auckland Radio – as well as Wellington. I heard Wellington put out a warning of tropical cyclone Dora. Well, I wasn't exactly in the tropics, and I hoped it would stay away from me.

As I was getting near land and expected shipping I stayed up all night at the tiller, and then turned in for no more than a couple of hours. I got up to a lovely day, although it was all light winds, and I was becalmed twice. I had one nasty fright. I was standing up in the bow, day-dreaming because it was such a beautiful day when suddenly I saw broken water ahead. My first thought was 'A reef!' and I raced back to the tiller. Then I saw that my 'reef' was an enormous whale, just breaking the surface. I breathed again.

The next few days were all calms and light airs, but they were days of lovely sunshine and I relaxed, feeling that I was having a sort of half-time break before the second half of the voyage. I saw my first fishing boat – or rather, his lights – on February 17th. On that day I finished my first tank of fresh water. It had lasted jolly well. I made a mental note to start collecting water next time there was any rain, but I had no immediate need of water and in that beautiful weather I didn't want to think of rain. I lay in the sun and read Agatha Christie.

On February 18th I decided that my break had lasted long

enough, and that I must get cracking again. It was still calm, but I tried to make use of every scrap of wind there was. New Zealand Radio put through three telephone calls to me and the New Zealand Cape Horners sent me a telegram saying 'Good luck. We admire your courage.' I was delighted with that.

A television crew came out to meet me in a boat called *Sea Witch*, and I spent half the night trying to bring her in on the radio for a rendezvous. They couldn't find me until midday, and then they interviewed me for TV. It was good to meet people again and we had a real party, although of course no one came on board. The TV crew had only spirits, so I gave them some of my Guinness. Usually it is the TV and Press men who give the beer away. It was a nice change to be on the giving side, particularly with cans that I'd transported myself halfway round the world.

But I was getting a bit tired of social life. No sooner had *Sea Witch* made off than I had three more telephone calls from the shore. It was nice to talk to people, and I couldn't help feeling a bit flattered that people should want to talk to me, but I couldn't spend all day answering the telephone. I wanted to get on, and that meant getting away from New Zealand. I was still having trouble with the halyards, and when I wanted to change the No 1 jib and tried to drop it, it jammed and I had to winch it down.

The calm weather went on. It was beautiful weather, really, but I was fed up with it, for I wanted wind. I had a nice telegram, which read 'From Otago yachtsmen. Fair winds and fast passage. Gordon Caly, President Otago Yachting Association.' I hoped that I'd soon get some of those fair winds.

Navigation was distinctly tricky. I was rounding the South Island of New Zealand, and saving time by cutting through the Foveaux Strait, a passage about twenty-five miles wide (at its narrowest) that separates South Island from the off-lying Stewart Island. There are islets and reefs in the passage, and I had to keep my eyes open. Sometimes it was so calm that I had barely steerage way, and this added to my difficulties – and frustration. I found myself getting childishly bad-tempered. On one occasion when a wave slopped on board and soaked me I tore off my soaked jumper and threw it into the sea, absolutely crying with rage. Afterwards I felt very much ashamed of myself.

Work was the best remedy for such tantrums, but with hot weather and next to no wind I didn't feel like work. I climbed the mast and tightened one of the crosstree struts, and listed a number of other maintenance jobs which needed doing, but I had to drive myself to get on with the maintenance when we were barely moving.

There were a number of fishing boats about, and sometimes they would come across for a chat. One, called the *Aygom,* was, I thought, the most beautiful fishing boat I'd ever seen. Her crew offered me some fish which I declined politely. They started to ask me about my Atlantic row but I believe the present is much more important than the past and I was on my way home! I couldn't hang about to tell them all about the row so I gave them my only copy of *A Fighting Chance,* the book of the Atlantic voyage which John Ridgway and I had written.

February 22nd brought the seventh day of calm. I spent most of the day at the tiller, with an interval when I climbed the mast to try to change the main halyard. I couldn't get it off, and had to add it to the list of things to be done.

Next morning gave me an easterly, which was just the wind I wanted to get through the strait. I ran down the coast for hours, looking at it through binoculars. It was a pleasant coast and reminded me of Scotland, but – perhaps oddly, after 128 days at sea – I didn't have the slightest desire to go ashore. I felt that I should like to visit New Zealand, but not then. All I wanted then was to press on.

That night, heading for Centre Island, I was startled by a fishing boat that came astern and started flashing its lights. The crew were also yelling at me, shouting what I thought was 'Reef!' I had main and mizzen goose-winged, and I dropped them both with some urgency. Then I discovered that the men were calling out 'TV', and were a television crew wanting an interview. Did I curse! I thought it was a fisherman warning me from his local knowledge that I was standing into danger.

During the night the wind veered to the south-west and I spent most of the night at the tiller, tacking back and forth. I felt boxed in, and I was very worried. I was not sure exactly where I was, for I was subject to a current and I didn't know just what it was doing. Towards morning it fell calm again, and I got a couple of hours' sleep. At dawn the TV boat came up to me again and they had their interview.

There followed a day and a night of winds all round the compass, sometimes reaching gale force. It meant another twenty-four hours at the tiller, and I began to feel very tired indeed. Things weren't made any easier by a ship going through the strait that refused to give way to me, so that I had to turn and run until she was clear. If I had kept my course she would have run me down.

With daylight I was able to identify Solander Island, at the western entrance to (from my point of view), the exit from the Foveaux Strait. I was north-east of Solander Island, and nearly through the strait. I had to pass Puysegur Point, on the mainland of South Island, and then I could reckon myself properly clear of the strait. It was blowing a full gale from the south, but at least it would get me clear. I made up my mind that once I'd cleared Puysegur Point I'd turn in and get my head down. I was quite desperate for sleep.

I slept all night, until about 04.00, when I woke because my sleeping bag was sopping. After the fine weather the leaks had opened up with a vengeance. It was blowing very hard. I looked at the wind indicator and the scale read 45 knots. Then I turned in again on the windward berth and I remember nothing more until 11.30. I must have been very tired.

When I did wake again I had a shock. A big wave, or more than one, must have hit us while I slept, for there was damage all over the place. The No 1 jib had broken out of its bag and was trailing in the sea; the halyards were broken, and the sail itself was badly torn. The much-mended running boom was broken again, although it had been lashed on deck. Below, the saloon was flooded. The electric pump wouldn't work, so I pumped by hand. Then I repaired the pump. My second tank of fresh water was still intact, but I couldn't get at the water because that pump was broken, too. Three food-bins had been split open, and the food was kept in place only because the side that had broken away had jammed on the battery box. The stern was a shambles. Kit had broken loose everywhere, and it took me three hours to sort it out. Not being able to get at the water tank I had to use my emergency supply. One good thing, however, came out of all the mess – I found some carrots I didn't know I had! At least, I thought that they were on board, but I had never been able to find them. The storm had found them for me.

I got another shock next morning when I looked at the mast – it had a terrific S-bend in it! I reduced sail at once, then studied the mast to see if I could discover what was wrong. The trouble seemed to be that the innermost starboard shroud was too tight. I tried to correct this with the bottlescrew, but I seemed only to make things worse. I'd have to go up the mast, but I couldn't attempt it there and then because the sea was much too rough. I could do nothing but carry on under a rag of sail, and pray. It stayed rough all day, but the evening brought a 'red sky at night', and although this hadn't worked when I was on the other side of New Zealand I hoped that being in the Tasman Sea might give a different result.

It did, at least on this occasion. The wind fell off during the night and by daybreak it was almost calm. I got on with fixing the mast at once. I had to climb to the top inner shroud and work my way out right to the end of the spreader. I was sitting in the bosun's chair working away quite happily when a squall came. Luckily it wasn't too bad, but to be up there rolling backwards and forwards, with the wind and rain howling round me was a terrifying experience. When the squall passed I went back to work. It was a tiresome job, but I managed to fix the shroud so that I could restore an even tension to it, and got the mast properly lined up again.

Next came the freshwater pump. My efforts here were defeated. I couldn't fix the pump because the end had broken off and I couldn't change over to the other pump because the hoses were too short. I could have opened the tank by lifting the lid, of course, but I didn't want to do this because the broken food bins were over the tank, and if I started lifting the lid their contents would spill all over the place. Since I couldn't think of any other way of getting at the water I decided to postpone the problem. The tank itself was intact, and the water inside it was safe enough. I could go on using my emergency water while it lasted, and hope to collect some more before it finished. If it didn't rain and I couldn't get any more fresh water, I'd have to get at the tank. But that problem was not immediate and for the moment it could wait.

I went round *British Steel* checking things and discovered that the bulb in the starboard navigation light had gone. And I found that I didn't have a spare! I could hardly believe it – it was about the only thing I had forgotten. I solved this problem by transferring the bulb from the stern light.

My next rendezvous for handing over mail and logs was in Storm Bay, Tasmania. I had hoped to make Tasmania from New Zealand in seven days, but with the time lost by having to reduce sail to save the mast, and in the calm that followed the storm I had to give up this hope. I reckoned, though, that I shouldn't be more than a day or so behind. Although there was always plenty to do I tried not to let a day pass without putting in some reading. This was partly for deliberate relaxation, partly to keep my mind alert. It was in the Tasman Sea that I read *The Strange Voyage of Donald Crowhurst*. I found this extraordinarily moving, and bits of it also made me angry. I wrote in my log at the time:

February 27th, 1971   Reading the book about Crowhurst. Sad – incredible. I wonder what would be said if I die – probably that I was unprepared or some such rot. The way things can be twisted! In the book he says that his navigating was a mite slapdash because he only took a sight in the morning, or the morning plus a noon sight using the short method. He rarely took simultaneous sights of stars and planets. The author, I would say, knows nothing of practical navigation. If he were to comment on mine it would look black indeed! Some days I don't take a sight for three or four days, and never, *never* have I taken one of the planets and stars. And I always use the short method. The truth is that when you have sea room you don't have to worry about navigation. If you know up to 20 – or even 100 – miles, there's no problem. It's people who talk about 'taking simultaneous sights of stars and planets' who put people off going on long passages. The idea should be to encourage such trips. It's a wonderful experience, a long passage, with or without a crew. I fully understand Moitessier saying that he wanted to save his soul. To some it appeared different. To them I say, 'Flash back to your office, your gin at night, your gossip, your scandal. You will never know the bliss of *almost* (I say *almost*) puritan outlook.'

Other jottings from my Tasman Sea log:

February 28th Heading for the rendezvous in Storm Bay. What a place for a rendezvous! It hasn't got that name for nothing! It's all indented from the Southern storms. Still, when I think of it this comes to mind—

> *When at last I sight the shore*
> *And the fearful breakers roar,*
> *Fear nought – He will pilot me.*

For lunch I had my Christmas chicken with roast potatoes and a glass of the vin rosé. I said a special grace.

Heard on Hobart Radio that they had a hailstorm. It will soon be winter here – the sun is almost all the way to start a North Declination. The great problem will be weathering the Cape of Good Hope.

Clock moved back one hour. Good news!

March 1st At 17.15 a very big raincloud passed overhead, then suddenly she backed to the south, then southeast. Then she passed downwind, and the wind, which was Force 5–6 dropped to only Force 2. I don't know why, but I suddenly felt frightened, very frightened. I dropped all sail as quickly as I could. I'm OK now, but I really felt as if something disastrous was going to happen. I've thought about it all, and I ask myself: If it had happened between Cape Horn and New Zealand, would I have dropped all sail? After all, the wind didn't go above Force 6, and I carry the main in that. The answer is No, I would not have dropped sail. I'd have kept going. Then why now? My own feeling is that it's coming in contact with people again. Somehow they've unsettled me.

I did feel strangely unsettled at this period of the voyage, and I could only put it down to meeting and talking to people off New Zealand. Yet I hadn't felt like that after meeting *Endurance* off Cape Horn. Perhaps this was because that meeting was short, and I was face to face with people only for a few minutes. The New Zealand meetings affected me quite differently; I felt that in some curious way they had slowed me down as a person, made me timid, and subject to wild imaginings. The prospect of my rendezvous off Tasmania began to worry me: I wanted to get it over as soon as possible. In fact, I felt that I didn't really want it at all. The one thing I did want was letters from Maureen; if it wasn't that the rendezvous would bring me her letters I might have cut it out altogether. If I'd done that, would people have said that I was mad?

These moods recurred at intervals, and I'd force myself to snap out of them. I'd been alone at sea for over four months – four months of my own thoughts, of unshared responsibility for my boat and for myself. I was not exactly misanthropic; I looked forward to the end of the voyage. But being near people while still on my voyage was like the difference between being safely in the open ocean and navigating near land. In the open sea one could feel safe; approaching land one was suddenly aware of all the hazards, of the things that *could* go wrong. I think this explains my sudden panic over the raincloud. It wasn't that I was afraid of anything in particular; I was just afraid. And I suppose that meeting the TV people and the fishermen off New Zealand, talking to men who had homes nearby, who would *go home* soon after they left me, to whom I was but an incident in normal life – I suppose all this had given me a kind of insecurity in my own existence, alone in a small boat with tens of thousands of miles still to cover before I could be at home. These feelings, which I tried to argue out with myself, taught me a lot, I think, about why men choose solitary avocations, become hermits, or go off on singlehanded adventures. They taught me too, perhaps, a good deal about myself. I was not sure that I liked it all. I learned at any rate that there were certain things against which I should have to be on guard.

I don't want to imply that I was constantly occupied with this sort of introspection. I wasn't. For the most part I thought of practical things – what sails to drop or set to get the best out of the yacht, the most profitable course to steer, how to tackle repair jobs, what to have for dinner. But a man can't be alone with himself without sometimes thinking deeply about life. I don't say that my thoughts were all that profound. But they are part of the record of my voyage.

I was often distressed by the news that the radio brought me; what a mess, what a mess so much of the world seemed to be in. I was particularly upset by the news from Northern Ireland, and when I heard of British soldiers being killed there I was sickened by the misery of it all. Why? Why? Why? What a stupid waste of all the opportunities for living. My heart went out to the soldiers, men I felt of as my mates. Nothing is worse than asking troops to do policing: it is a thankless, bitter task. I hated to think of what the Army was going through in Northern Ireland.

I reflected on the future. What was my own future going to be? I didn't (and don't) know. I set down some of my thoughts in a letter (to be picked up at the rendezvous) to Phil Wolfinden.

After nine years in the Paras (I wrote) the only thing I can say I'm good at is this sort of thing. Paras don't actugive you a good grounding for civilian life – there are very few vacancies for hired guns or trained killers.

I thought rather bitterly about the reluctance of so many British firms to take on new people. My letter went on

The sad thing about the UK is that companies won't

take a chance on new blood or thinking. In America a person may change his profession three or four times in his life – in the UK, once an accountant, always an accountant. Unless you've had 99 years as a clerk, they don't want you as a possible tea-boy.

Is this fair? Perhaps it reflected my own rather hard struggle in life since I was sixteen. I'd seen men in jobs which I knew I could do, but which I also knew I'd never be given a chance to do. And I'd resented it. Yet I could scarcely complain about being given *no* chances – I'd been given *British Steel*, and that was a wonderful chance. Of course I'd worked to be where I was and doing what I wanted, sailing singlehanded in the Tasman Sea, on my way home from circumnavigating the world. But I owed a lot to other people's readiness to take a chance – on me. I tried to say thank you to Phil—

There is no doubt in my mind whatsoever that without you we should never, *never* have been ready in time. It was your never-failing loyalty to the project and endless efforts that got me off on October 18th. I cannot find the vocabulary to express my gratitude.

I had a particular problem of gratitude to Frank Allen. When my self-steering gear went near the Horn and I'd radioed the news back home, Frank had at once had a new part made and suggested that it should be sent out to one of my rendezvous. I didn't want it. This was not being ungrateful to Frank – I was very, very grateful to him. But I wanted to get round the world with the gear I'd started with; if it broke or went wrong, it was up to me to mend or make do by my own efforts. If anything had gone so seriously wrong that I'd had to put in somewhere, I'd certainly have had the self-steering gear repaired. But as long as I could

keep going, well, I wanted to keep going. I hope that Frank
and everybody else concerned with trying to help me under-
stands this. I think they do.

On March 2nd I was 110 miles from Tasmania, and
becalmed. If it hadn't been for that calm I'd still have had a
chance of making Tasmania from New Zealand in seven
days, but the calm then dished my chances. There was a
'high' settled over Tasmania. There was nothing I could do
about it, and that was that. I got on with writing letters to be
handed over at the rendezvous and stood myself a whisky.

The calm continued. My log notes:

March 3rd What a drag – it's now 13.00. I'm going
nowhere. Another 'high' over Tasmania. I'd rather have
gales than this. If anything annoys me more, it's calms.
They are OK if you are not in a hurry, but I am. Every
day the sun gets farther north, and the weather will get
very much worse.

It's really a pity I've got to go to Tasmania. I really
would like to forget it, but for that letter from Maureen. I
must own it will be great to read all the news. I worry
about her and Samantha.

A plane flew overhead taking photographs. I had a reef
in the main – I could imagine his saying, 'He's not taking
any chances!' Actually, it's sometimes better to have the
reef in. I get better balance that way. Not to worry – it will
give the Harbour Stallions something to criticize!

I tried to make a radio telephone call to Peter Jones-
Evans, who'd been best man at my wedding and who had
settled in Tasmania. I got through, but learned that he
would not be home until evening. Later I did get him, and
we had a wonderful yarn. He'd become a manager with his
company, and was doing well. It was great to be able to talk
to him.

This conversation with Peter put me in good spirits and,
o top it all, the radio operator came from Edinburgh. He
aid my operating was 'quite good'. (But, being a Scot,
perhaps he had to say that!)

After my radio call I went back to the tiller, to nurse
British Steel along at about 2 knots in such wind as there
was. It was a lovely night, but I got fed up with it. I went
below and had fried rice with curry powder and a tin of my
precious prawns. And I had a Drambuie.

All next day (March 4th) it was calm. I did absolutely
nothing, but just rested, and felt the better for it. At 20.00
hours a wind got up from the north-east and I was off. I
radioed to change the rendezvous from the bay to a position
off Cape Raoul, because the north-east wind made the bay
a lee shore. I made the rendezvous at 08.05 hours on March
5th. The last entry in the log I handed over reads:

> *March 4th* I have two problems, on top of the winds
> and currents, against me. 1. The southerly busters. 2.
> Weathering the Cape of Good Hope. God willing, I'll
> make it.

CHAPTER SIX

The Worst Ocean

On leaving Tasmania there was a different feel to my voyage. *British Steel* had carried me halfway round the rim of the world, and although I had still the other half to sail I could feel that I was homeward bound. My next great milestone was the Cape of Good Hope – once round that I should be in waters that Maureen and I had sailed together. The Cape of Good Hope might still be a long way off, but I was properly on my way there.

I could not know that by far the worst stage of the voyage was ahead of me, and I left the rendezvous off Tasmania feeling cheerful. I had a big bundle of letters to read and Mrs Parker, the wife of the contact man for the rendezvous, had sent me a bunch of flowers. I put them in the galley, and they seemed to brighten up the whole ship.

Meeting people off Tasmania did not leave me as unsettled as I was after the rendezvous off New Zealand. Perhaps this was because the meeting was shorter – it was all over in about two hours. Even so, it was a longer halt than I wanted, though it was my own fault for talking too much!

I left with a good easterly wind blowing at 25 knots and it was nice to run for a change. I stayed at the tiller through the rest of the day, but at last I couldn't keep awake any longer and had to go below to get some sleep. Apart from two hours at the rendezvous, I had been at the tiller continuously for

venty-seven hours and I was very tired. Before turning in I
adioed Hobart to give my position and I was told that Mel-
ourne wanted to speak to me. When I got through, my
rother Robert was waiting to talk to me! He had been in
ustralia for three years, and was doing well. It was great to
e able to speak to him.

I woke next morning (March 6th) to find myself all but
ecalmed. The weather report offered me a Force 3, but it
as more like Force 0. I re-read all my letters. It was super to
ave news of Maureen and everyone, and there was a lovely
hotograph of Samantha – I thought 'My, but she's grown!'
 letter that gave me particular pleasure was from the pupils
f Primary 7 of Trinity School, Hawick. It was good of them
 write, and I should like them to know how much their
tter meant to me.

I considered tactical planning for my navigation to the
ape of Good Hope. Should I go north, to about 40°S,
nd sail nearer to the Australian coast? or should I stay
round 45°S until I was within striking distance of the
ape? I decided to stay south, unless bad weather forced
e north.

The next few days were mostly calm and I made little
rogress. To prevent myself from getting slack and not
othering to set sails to make the most of every breath of
ind, I re-read the letter from Primary 7 of Trinity School. I
ouldn't help but do my best after reading that letter. I wrote
 my log: 'If children get pleasure from following this trip
en suddenly it all becomes much more worth while. It gives
e real pleasure to know that they are enjoying the
oyage.'

I had a good laugh at Melbourne Radio. The operator
ame up with the usual weather report and at the end he
aid, 'Will those yachts on their way to Port Philip please
eport in and give positions and ETA. I'm getting calls
om anxious girls!' Then the air was full of call signs from

yachts, obviously all concerned in case their girl was among the anxious ones!

I heard a record of Johnny Ray's which brought back a flood of memories from my schooldays, in particular of one concerning a horse. Ever since a nasty incident with a horse when I was a child I've had a great fear of horses, and I won't go near a horse at any price. One day I was out for a walk with a girl called Peggy and we crossed a field with a horse in it. Suddenly it began to gallop towards us. 'Let's run,' I said. 'Oh no, it's OK,' said Peggy. But I wasn't waiting – I was off. When the horse got to Peggy it stopped, and she stood stroking it. She looked around for her would-be knight – and he was on the other side of the fence. Peggy saw the funny side of it, and went into near hysterics. I didn't think it at all amusing.

On March 9th I listened on the radio to the Frazier-Clay fight. I found it gripping and I suppose like millions of others I was disappointed when Clay didn't win. To me he will always be the greatest, and to make a comeback as he did showed him to be some man.

It was foggy for much of that day but by late afternoon the sun came out. The wind stayed light but with the evening a great bank of cloud appeared and I felt that we were in for a blow. It didn't come, and I had to stay tensed with waiting through all that night and the next day. It's hateful to be waiting for a gale. When you have been in one for a time, it's OK, but waiting for a gale to start is a really fearful feeling. On March 10th I covered only forty-four miles, but the next day brought wind, Force 5–6 from the west. It was good to be on the move again, and away we went south-west, with a reef in the main, No 2 boomed foresail and mizzen. Later the wind backed to the south-west and I was able to head almost due west.

The radio that day brought dreadful news from Northern Ireland. It made me sick and angry and I wrote at the time:

Heard about the three soldiers being shot through the head. I prayed for the boys' parents.

The wind did not last and *British Steel* was soon slatting about again in light airs and near calm. But the sea was anything but smooth, with big, confused rollers left by past squalls. I decided to stop listening to the radio. I fiddled at the tiller for hour after hour to try to keep the yacht moving until I got so frustrated that I decided to drop all the sails and go to sleep. While thinking about which one to drop I somehow started to sing a nursery rhyme, one which Samantha and I used to sing together: 'Here we go round the mulberry bush . . .' I immediately thought of her and the last time we sang it together. I said to myself, 'There's a little girl waiting there, waiting for her daddy.' That hardened my resolve to keep going, and the sails stayed up.

I decided to make myself a cup of tea, and this led to a chain of trouble, laughable now, but maddening at the time. I still couldn't get water from the water-tank, and I'd been using my emergency supply. Now that was finished, so I *had* to get water from the tank. I had a small emergency water pump, and to get at the tank I used this pump to pump water into a container. Because the pump hadn't been used it was rather oily, and my tea turned out to be distinctly oily. But I couldn't afford to throw away any water, so I drank the tea as it was and thought it was hellish. This incident, however, made me think, and I realized that I had broken an extremely basic rule – by using up my emergency water supply I had left myself no water in containers, so that if I had to abandon ship I'd have no water to take with me to the life-raft. This wouldn't do at all, and I knew that I'd *got* to do something about it. The realization must have put some compartment of my brain to work, for suddenly I thought of a way of transferring water from the tank I couldn't get at properly to the empty tank with the good pump. The little emergency pump was no good – it would make all the water oily, and it would be dreadfully slow. *But I had a portable bilge pump*! That would do the job quite satisfactorily, and I'd make sure that a container was kept full of water in case of some real emergency.

Squalls and unsteady winds continued. I lost all the elation I'd had on leaving Tasmania and felt increasingly depressed. I didn't like this part of the ocean at all. There was something infinitely bleak about it – range after range of rollers, with long valleys between them, giving an impression of the bleaker parts of Dartmoor. I was still pretty far south, about 44° S, and it was getting colder with the approach of autumn in this part of the world. There were two nasty incidents during squalls, when the wind suddenly backed and *British Steel* was brought up all standing, with her sails aback. She took it well, and fortunately came through without damage, but it was worrying.

I wasn't feeling at my best, and was concerned about suffering from fatigue or mental 'plonk'. One particular incident brought me up sharply. I got a time signal on the radio, started my stopwatch and went to get my sextant – instead, I opened the oven door and stood for two full minutes looking into the oven! Then I said, aloud, 'What the hell are you looking in the oven for?' I had to think seriously for another couple of minutes before I remembered that I wanted the sextant to go and get a sight. To snap out of whatever was affecting me I wrote out a list of jobs that needed doing. These were:

1 Change main halyard
2 Patch main
3 Patch mizzen

I made up my mind to seek a little northing in the hope of slightly warmer weather, but I didn't want to go north of 40° S. On March 16th Sydney Radio put out a warning of

destructive winds up to 70 knots'. Sydney was over 1,000
miles away, but I gave them a call, and to my astonishment
they answered! It turned out that the winds were not in my
area. The radio contact was remarkably good – about the
best I'd had in 800 miles.

I hadn't had a proper wash for what seemed ages because of
the water situation, but now that was fixed I decided that I
needed a good clean up. So I had a wash and shave, put on
clean clothes, and threw the old stuff over the side. Immediately I felt better. I sent a telegram to the British Steel Corporation via Adelaide, asking 'Would you like my ETA,' I
nearly collapsed with laughing after I'd sent it, and imagined
Maureen saying 'He's getting too cocky.' But I had to have
an ETA so why not give one, even though I was still half
the world away from home?

On March 19th I had a bit of luck. I went to get a steak
and kidney pie from my stores, and to get at it I had to take
out my fishing kit. Underneath this, on the bottom shelf of
the locker, there was some brown paper covering something.
I took out the brown paper – *and there was some lighter
fuel*! How I wished I could have found it in the Cape Horn
days when it was so bitterly cold and I was seriously short of
matches. Anyway, I didn't have to worry about the match
shortage any more. The sea soon puts you in your place,
though. Just after I'd found the lighter fuel we luffed to one
side and a bottle of tomato ketchup went from the galley
underneath the chart table, sending red ketchup all over the
place. It managed to get everywhere, over the bulkhead and
into the cabin. It was a vile job to get it cleaned up.

The log shows my ups and downs of mood over this
period.

March 20th Contacted Perth and arranged new sched-
ules for the next three weeks. I've now mentally prepared

myself for a long haul to South Africa. The winds are just not constant, seas bumpy, and it's a drag. But I'll get there one day!

March 21st I'm very concerned about the sails – they are in a bad way. If only I could get a calm – I just won't stop as long as there is wind.

If anyone had seen me tacking I'd have been certified insane. Crashing through the seas, spray coming, and waves right over us. I stood by the mizzen, singing at the top of my voice and also dancing (but holding on always). Then I'd make like to whip *Brit,* and I'd shout 'Come on *Brit,* show me the way home.' It's just that after such lousy winds I'm so pleased to be on the move, even if it is a gale.

March 22nd The sails were dropped at 12.00 approx. Reason – rollers. I've never experienced them like this before. I should think they are about 20–30 feet high, but with no long valleys in between as you get with a swell. They are on you in quick succession. The wind is from the south-east, light, Force 1–2, and as the rollers press under you get a back draught, and the top goes into spray. It produces a very odd feeling. You are completely at the mercy of the rollers – having no sail up, you have no control. I hate this place only because of the lack of consistency.

I think today is the first time I've felt really lonely. I've thought of Samantha and Maureen all day long. These moods are not good. They don't last long, but I feel so sad, chiefly at knowing how futile a struggle it would be if it was decided that I should die. You cannot but be impressed by the enormity of the whole – sea, waves, sky, it's all very big and overpowering.

March 23rd Wind from the north-east, Force 4. I've been on the tiller all day. No matter how I try, I can't get her to run with a lashed tiller, or even with it free. Of course the wind is unsteady, and that doesn't help. It's the inconsistency of the winds that makes it so tiring. It is no longer a physical *and* mental effort, it is *only* mental. It's hard, and very frustrating. Physically it's not hard work, really – I've known it a lot worse. As long as the mind doesn't give up – the mind always packs up before the body.

I came prepared for eighteen months, so store-wise I'm OK. I've been lulled into thinking it was easier by getting from the Horn to New Zealand in fifty-six days. Still, I look on that as a bonus. Collected approx five gallons of water.

March 24th Beginning to notice what an important factor food has become. I think what I'm going to have for the next meal almost immediately I finish the previous one. Not hunger or greed – just distraction. Often it's the case that when I say I'll have something, I forget what I was going to have and end up with something else.

Just heard that Frank Sinatra has retired; pity, he really is a fantastic entertainer. He will be missed, he has given pleasure to millions.

March 25th Put a couple of stitches in the main where it was parting. The needle went off the metal palm just as I was pressing it with all my might. Result – it pierced into my hand, making a stab wound. It went about halfway in. I put TCP and a dressing on, but it's sore, and it's swelling a little. I hope it doesn't get poisonous. It would be awkward.

March 26th What a find! I was raking about in the workroom cupboards, looking in the boxes for a split pin, and at the very bottom I found a big box of biscuits. Wonderful! I thought I had only one box, and that went a long time ago. Biscuits with morning coffee now.

One of the jobs that I'd given myself to do some days ago,

when I'd found myself staring into the oven without know
ing why, was to replace the main halyard. This had been
worrying me more and more, because it was suffering badly
from chafe. But in spite of my good resolution I hadn't been
able to do anything about it because of the weather; when
there was no wind there were gigantic rollers, and when
there was wind it was too rough to think of going up the
mast. On the same day that I found the biscuits – March
26th – my chance came. The wind fell away, and although
there was still a heavy swell, conditions seemed about as
good as they were ever likely to be. I planned the job as
carefully as I could before I started, working out precisely
how to ensure that I wouldn't get the new halyard tangled
up with the old one. I thought over all the tools I should
need, so that I wouldn't find myself at the masthead lacking
the right spanner. Then I went up.

I couldn't use the bosun's chair because of the amount of
stays and tangs at the top. A chair could not be hoisted high
enough. I had to stand and hang on to get at the halyard
block. The whole job took 1¾ hours: and it was no joke to
cling to a sixty-foot pendulum while undoing a bolt with
two spanners, one to hold and the other to loosen the nut.
However, with slow determination I held on and got the job
done. While I was up there I discovered that the No 1 halyard block had been chafing on the mast and had almost
worn a hole through the metal. There was nothing whatever
I could do about it, except to pray that it would hold for
about another 14,000 miles.

My speedometer had packed up soon after I left Tasmania – probably, I thought, because of barnacles. It wasn't
all that necessary to me because by this time I could estimate
British Steel's speed fairly well, so I didn't bother about it. I
think, though, that I usually tended to underestimate our
speed (subconsciously perhaps deliberately so, because of
the bonus it gave me when I worked out a sight and found

our true position!). I got three good sights on the day of my work on the halyard, and got a remarkably small triangle, considering how I was being rocked about by the swell. They put me at 38° 20′S, 116°E. I'd have preferred to be a bit farther south, but it couldn't be helped, for the wind largely dictated where I went. Otherwise, I was pleased with the position, for it gave me quite a bonus towards South Africa from where I'd reckoned to be. It also made it possible for me to change on to my last chart of the Southern Ocean. But I didn't get out the new chart straightaway; these charts overlap a bit, and I thought I'd stay on the old one as long as I could to give myself a good start on the new one! Silly? Looking back, perhaps so, but at the time these little games were important to me, and I think they played a real part in helping to keep up my spirits. A singlehander almost *must* play games with himself if he is to keep on top of things and not let things get on top of him.

To celebrate the successful completion of the job on the halyard I stood myself a haggis for supper, and also opened a new bottle of Scotch – my third since I started (not exactly heavy drinking, for I made a bottle last something like two months). I paid for my self-indulgence by developing a pain in my tummy. I don't think this was due either to the haggis or the Scotch, but to a jar of pickles which I hadn't touched for ages. I thought they didn't taste too good, but rashly ignored the warning. The pain bothered me for about twenty-four hours, but yielded to a meal of custard, which seemed to settle my stomach.

Around midnight on the night of March 27th–28th there was a particularly fierce squall, with the wind suddenly rising to Force 10. I had to drop all sail as quickly as I could. While I was securing the sails I heard a sudden hissing, and a great wave engulfed the yacht from bow to stern. I jammed myself between two sails which were packed and secured, and clung to the stays as the sea swept over me. Amazingly there seemed to be no damage.

The weather continued rough, with wildly inconstant winds. I started the new chart, which actually showed South Africa, but the distance seemed so vast that I folded the chart in three so that it did not look so horrifying. My tummy having recovered, I thought I'd have a Christmas pudding, and to save water I steamed it over salt water. It was not wholly successful, for during the steaming process we were hit by a squall, and a good deal of salt water got into the pudding. I improved things by pouring a miniature bottle of brandy over the pudding, and the result was eatable and, indeed, not too bad. While eating my pudding we had an entertaining encounter with an albatross. *British Steel* was going along at about 4 knots and an albatross decided to land right in her path. We were almost on top of him as he touched down. To take off again he had to have a run to get airborne, and he made a frantic effort to run sideways on the same course as us. I couldn't do anything to help, because we were so nearly on top of him that any change of course might have engulfed him more seriously. As it was, I don't suppose that he was in much real danger, and his antics to take off were slapstick comedy. He got away in the end, and the affair gave me a good laugh.

On April 1st I sent a telegram to the British Steel Corporation giving my ETA at the Hamble as August 7th. At the time I rather hoped they'd realize that it was All Fools Day; but I was at least half serious, because I'd done my arithmetic very carefully. As things turned out I got home on August 6th.

But I was a long way from August 6th when I sent that telegram, and the thought chiefly in my mind was whether barnacles were going to have a really serious effect on *British Steel*. They'd been noticeable for some time, and I felt that they were definitely slowing us up. On April 2nd I went over the side to have a look. It was too cold to go in bare, so I went in my diving suit. I was shocked by what I saw. There seemed to be an enormous amount of barnacles, all about six inches long, clinging to *British Steel*. With a short breather, I stayed in the water for nearly two hours, trying to clean barnacles from the hull, but I made next to no impression on them. Back on board again I pondered what to do. If barnacles were costing me 1 knot in speed, that would be twenty-four miles a day and 168 miles a week – appalling thought. I considered whether I could possibly find somewhere to beach *British Steel* to clean the hull, but soon ruled that out. Barnacles were most serious in light airs, so the best bet seemed to be to stay as far south as I could, where it was liable to be rough. Apart from that there didn't seem much that I could do, except be patient.

Patience was peculiarly difficult just then because I was much worried about Maureen. To give myself a particular treat I'd booked a radio-telephone call to Maureen for April 3rd. I was very excited, and shaved carefully the night before, because I couldn't possibly take a phone call from Maureen with a beard! My log describes my feelings at the time.

April 3rd (Saturday) At 10.07 GMT Maureen came on the line and gave me the latest news. It was wonderful to hear her, and I felt very full – she sounded so depressed. I think the waiting is beginning to wear her down a little – no wonder. I know people will continually ask her about the trip, and that doesn't help. Samantha next – what a joy to hear her. True to form, she reminded me to bring home the present which I'd promised. After talking for six minutes we left. Then after half an hour I thought, 'To hell with it,' and phoned her again. Unfortunately she had just gone out, so I spoke to Maureen's mother, who told me that Maureen was sad at my being away and, in fact, the call had upset her. It would have been better not to call. Well, I've arranged a schedule for tomorrow. I can't leave her feeling depressed.

April 4th Tried to contact Maureen. Unfortunately she was out (I had not alerted her I was going to call). Will try again tomorrow.

April 5th Phoned Maureen. Found out she hadn't been well, and the doctor has advised a holiday. I'm pleased she's going for one with May (a friend of hers) so I know she'll get some rest. She told me my sister Isabel has had a baby boy and she has called him Chay. I'm looking forward to seeing him.

I taped my conversation with Maureen so now when I want to hear her, all I do is play it back. Pity Samantha was off to nursery, or I could have recorded her as well.

The radio-telephone is a marvellous invention, and it has given almost a new dimension to long voyages in small boats. But I'm not sure that it always adds to happiness; it can also make for anxiety. Without radio, a lone sailor would disappear for months, suffering heartache, maybe, at being cut off so completely from those he loves, but more able to adjust himself philosophically to separation. So with those at home – they know that months must elapse before there is any hope of news, and they, too, can adjust themselves to waiting. Radio can bring wonderful encouragement – but actually to talk to someone you love, knowing that an ocean lies between you, sometimes makes separation seem even sharper. Those calls to Maureen meant much to me; whether they were really kind to her I am less sure. Thinking on these things now simply adds to my conviction that my voyage was a far harder task for Maureen than it was for me. And it makes me still more conscious of my immeasureable debt to her.

*   *   *

Work (as always) was the best antidote to depressing thoughts. I couldn't do much about the barnacles, but I could do everything possible to keep *British Steel* moving. If that meant apparently endless hours at the tiller, and ever-lasting sail-changing to make the most of the inconstant winds, well, so it had to be. I felt the loss of the self-steering gear more now than at any time since it had broken off Cape Horn. And for some reason at this stage of the voyage I wasn't physically at my best. Whether this was the cumulative effect of fatigue, or whether the long haul to South Africa was a sort of emotional anticlimax to the slog from the Horn to New Zealand, I don't know, but I had to drive myself to get things done. I paid for my feeling of lethargy on April 8th. I woke soon after midnight that morning to a rising wind. I could hear it blowing as I lay in my bunk, and I knew that I ought to get up and go on deck, but I didn't. I lay there for at least an hour, simply listening to the wind, and willing it to moderate. The wind took no notice, and at 02.45 I knew that I had to get up. I dressed quickly and went out to drop the main. The wind pressure on the sail was terrific, forcing it to stay up, and I had to fight to get it down. The struggle left my hands and arms aching, and I did what I had never done before – I left the sail as it was and went into the cockpit for about five minutes for a breather. Always before this I had never left a sail until it was wrapped up properly and secured. This time I just didn't bother.

When I went back to the sail the wind was trying to tear it apart. My practice in bundling up a sail was to keep very low on the deck, hunching myself right over the sail and boom. I used to try to jam myself in somehow, using the lashed-down boom for support. *This time I hadn't lashed the boom.*

What happened next is not in my log. I left it out delib-erately, because I thought that my logbook might be

collected at a rendezvous off South Africa and get home
before me, and I didn't want Maureen to know how nearly
she became a widow that night. But I described the incident
in a letter to Frank Allen (with strict instructions not to
tell Maureen).

Dear Frank,

Very difficult to answer your letter at present – I'm
absolutely punch-drunk – this is not in my logs and please
don't tell Maureen. I kid you not, on an occasion such as
has just passed I'm knocked silly – how the hell the yacht
has taken it is beyond my comprehension.

About two days ago (I can't remember which day without looking up my log) Maureen was almost a widow and
again this isn't in my log . . .

I didn't have a safety-harness on (this is happening too
often, forgetting to put it on). And I'd forgotten to lash
down the after end of the boom. At this stage you have to
try to think of her crashing against the oncoming waves,
the boom banging and pitching up and down, the yacht
heeling to 35 deg. Also you have the waves' unhindered
sweep across the deck. Well, one nasty one hit me. I took
its weight on the boom, but the boom moved and I was
thrown to the lee side where the water was roaring along,
with the lee rail under. I lay amongst the water, luckily
pressed against the stanchion. I had to *scale* the deck, like
climbing a cliff, to get up windward.

This incident shook me. It was not the danger; oddly,
perhaps, I was not particularly frightened – it was almost as
if I were resigned to my fate, if I was to go, I'd go, so to
speak. But it was a survival situation, what I was really there
for, and it showed what happens if ever you let self-
discipline slip. I had to recognize that I was subject to a

continuous wearing-down process. It was like being knocked down every time you stand up, with sandpaper rubbing away at you all the time as well. Every time *British Steel* took off from a wave I was left tense, and waiting for the crash. Every time I made a movement I had to hang on; if I leant against something, my weight forced against it, and if there was a sharp projection, it dug into me. Everything about the yacht was damp and uncomfortable. Before, I had just accepted damp as something inevitable, but now it seemed to soak into my very being. All my clothes itched with damp. It was easy to feel sorry for myself, but fortunately I could recognize these symptoms of fatigue and stiffen my will to guard against them. I told myself that my job was to hang on and drive *British Steel* to the Cape of Good Hope. Once I'd turned the corner there I could look forward to the Trades – to flying fish, dolphins, perhaps to mermaids sitting under umbrellas drinking ice-cold Pepsi and waving to me as I went by. 'Get to the Trades,' I said, 'and all will be sweet and well. One day I *will* turn right.' So I forced myself to keep going.

My far from successful work on barnacles had at least got the speedometer going again, although I was pretty sure that it was under-registering. This gave me a pleasant surprise on April 9th, when a sight put me eighty miles farther west than I'd thought. Easter Sunday (April 11th) gave me a good day's sailing, although I had to spend most of it at the tiller. Being Easter Sunday I went to my 'master book' to find out where my Easter Special Pack was. The index said 'P35'. So I turned to P35 and read, 'Easter Pack – sorry, darling, I forgot to make it up. M.' I had to laugh, but I wasn't going to be outdone. Maureen, I thought, may have forgotten Easter, but she won't have forgotten her birthday. I reckoned that I'd be home before her birthday, so I found her Birthday Special Pack and opened that. In it was a cake, a tin of ham, a tin of rhubarb, a tin of sausages, a miniature bottle of brandy and a game of puzzles. That gave me my Easter feast.

The week after Easter was not a very happy one. My log recalls:

April 13th Fog most of the day – it's miserable weather. I'm really feeling tired, and I'm definitely lagging. I wonder if I should increase my vitamin tablets? Half the day I'm in a trance, and a lot of things are mechanical. I find I'm moving on deck a lot without my harness – very foolish. I must be aware all the time. I hobble along the deck like an old man – this is due to lack of exercise, I feel. Contrary to what some people feel, you don't get stronger, but weaker. Back is continually sore, and the cold persists.

Even at the time this self-pity irritated me. My log entry for that day concludes:

Blimey, listen to that whining! You'll think I'm a hospital case! Anyway, can't be much wrong – I've eaten half of Betty's cake, also the tin of ham, with roast potatoes for supper.

That week went on:

April 14th I've finished my nuts – they will be missed. I got a 7 lb bag from the staff of the Marine Hotel at Dartmouth. Also the chewing gum is finished.

Thick fog all day.

April 15th 41° 10′S, 78° 10′E. A sudden bang, and then the banging and clatter of sails woke me. A quick flash, and I suspected the halyard for the No 2. I was wrong, it was the block at the masthead which had parted.

I dropped the No 2, packed it away and hoisted the No 3 (it was squally, NW Force 5–6) but I had to get something up, and I'd no halyard for the No 1 or 2, so it was up No 3.

By 10.00 it was calm and pouring with rain. I took the No 2 halyard off – now I'm using the No 3 for all the foresails. I'll get another halyard up once round the corner. I don't fancy going up the mast in this swell.

Should have contacted Cape Town, but couldn't raise them.

April 16th Great NW wind – give me more, I love it.

I'm just on the edge of the Ice Zone – I'd like to get a little farther north.

April 17th Thick fog in the early part of the morning, but cleared as the barometer dropped and the wind got up from Force 4 to Force 8.

Dropped the main at 15.15. At 18.30 I changed from No 2 to No 3. I certainly miss the other halyard – having to change the shackle over, and make sure it's running straight all takes time.

While I was changing the No 2 I was up in the bow, and I heard a hissing. I knew what it was – a wave about to strike. Normally I just hold on and crouch. For some reason, this time I turned to see it. I saw it all right – it smashed into me, forcing me back and I just sat down as if I'd sat in a chair. But no chair, and I was soaked. No idea of the height, but a lot taller than I am, and I was in the bow. I suppose about 15–20 feet.

I was now just over halfway between Australia and South Africa. Getting to the Cape of Good Hope so dominated my thinking that I thought oddly little about the rest of the long way home. 'Once we've weathered the Cape', I kept telling myself, 'all will be well.' When I did think of the passage homeward after I'd turned the corner, my main concern was the problem of getting *British Steel* to steer herself when running. I had neither self-steering gear nor good running booms. So far I'd not had much success. I could get the yacht to hold a course well enough when on the wind, but running meant hour after hour at the tiller. If the trade wind was to blow me home in good time I'd have to do better than I'd managed up to now, for having to steer the yacht by hand would hold me up. With a crew, it wouldn't have mattered; there would have been someone to relieve me when I needed sleep. But a singlehander without self-steering is at a sad disadvantage; he *has* to have sleep, and if he can't get his boat to steer herself he must heave-to and lose precious miles when he leaves the helm. The problem of the trade wind, however, was still some way ahead. All I could do was to go on experimenting.

My immediate problem as we crawled over the apparently endless chart towards South Africa was to maintain self-discipline and combat lethargy. April 20th was windless and I spent the whole day on personal and ship maintenance. First I gave myself a haircut and a thoroughly good wash, including my hair, and then inspected myself like a mother inspecting a new-born baby. Apart from a couple of salt-water sores, which were not particularly bad, I passed myself fit. Then I went up the mast to clear a fouling halyard at the top jumpers. With no wind I had no sail to steady the yacht, and the pendulum-swing at the masthead as she rolled in the swell was horrible. However I got the job done, and turned next to sorting out the jib sheets, which were becoming badly frayed at the ends. No matter how well I whipped them, the whipping always seemed to come off. I tried a new method this time, and hoped for better results.

I saw three whales, and listened to a Scottish Half Hour on the radio. It was good to hear my native songs. All in all, that was one of my better days on this long haul of the voyage.

CHAPTER SEVEN

Storm

It was as well that that calm day came when it did, for the next month was a succession of storms, worse than anything I'd met in any other ocean of the world. It was not a good time of year, for winter was coming on. Of course, I'd reckoned on this when planning the voyage, but the reality was far more horrible than anything I had imagined. There was a peculiar quality of venom in the seas, a viciousness that I'd not experienced even in the lonely wastes south of Cape Horn. I know that the sea is neutral in human affairs, that when the wind lashes waves to fury it is utterly impersonal. But it doesn't feel like that: alone in a fierce sea you feel that the ocean is making a determined effort to get *you*. Man is pitifully small against such gigantic forces. You feel over and over again that it is only by God's will that you survive.

My recollection of the weeks between April 20th and May 21st, when I rounded Cape Agulhas (to the east of the Cape of Good Hope, and actually the southernmost point of Africa) is of continuous squalls and heavy seas. My log reminds me that there were interludes when conditions were better, and since memory is fickle I'll leave the narrative of this period mostly to the log. It begins with the storm that followed my day of calm.

*　　　*　　　*

April 21st It's now 20.00 hrs. I'd best write the log now – I may not be around in the morning. (Only slightly joking!)

I got up at 07.00 and by 09.30 the wind was Force 6–7, with the barometer 1013. It's now Force 8–9, gusting 10, and the barometer is 1008, and falling.

This is a very fierce storm; things have gone flying – cups, knives, even the frying pan. At one stage we got hit with I don't know what, and I seriously thought I'd collided with something. I keep leaving the tops of waves and dropping like a stone. I'm grateful it's dark so I can't see what the seas are like.

I'm not sure if I'm keeping the sail up to keep on the move, or if I'm too frightened to go on deck. This is a bad one. I'm feeling a little apprehensive. (What an understatement!) We keep luffing up, and what a racket! You'd think the heavens were falling in. (They very well could be.)

I took three films today inside the cabin and I had to use the lights, special high power things. Result, they've left the batteries flat. With a contact due tomorrow with Cape Town that's not good, because if the weather doesn't go down I won't be able to charge the batteries, or even run the engine while I'm transmitting.

As we go over on our side the water from the bilges (though I've pumped them out) keeps getting forced through the floor joins. If it gets worse I'll have to lie a-hull. I might even have to turn and run – that would break my heart. We've had lots of Force 8–9–10 before, but never with such venom as this one. The waves are really crashing hard against us. I suppose it's madness to keep going with only 2,000 miles to go.* I can't help it, I have to press on. Really, when it comes to it, this is what

---

* ie, to the Cape.

it's all about. The cockpit has been filled a dozen times. Attack!

April 22nd 01.50 Barometer 1000 and dropping. I have a minor problem. I'm locked in! I shut the door before getting into my sleeping bag (because of the cockpit being flooded) and the sheets have got under the teak grating in the cockpit and I can't open the door. So I went to the forehatch, but it's been so long since I opened it that that, too, was stuck. So here I am with a very expensive coffin. Anyway, with a hammer and a bar I got the forehatch open, but the boomed foresail is sheeted in tight, and I can't open the hatch fully. So when the time comes to get out I'll have to cut the sheet from the boomed foresail – I hope I won't have to get out before daylight.

Cabin floor is flooded. No juice in the batteries to pump it out, and I can't get to the pump in the cockpit.

18.00 Well, at 03.45 it just stopped blowing. Then came a zephyr of a breeze, but with the waves from the gale it was impossible to sail, so all sail down, and bed. I didn't get going until 11.30. This was directly after a contact with Cape Town Radio – my, but it was good to hear them. I made a schedule for a weekly contact.

The storm took its toll – the topping lift for the mizzen, and the spare halyard which ran through the sheave at top of the mast (damn nuisance this – if the last halyard parts now I haven't a spare until I can get up the mast). Two bad tears in mizzen, batten from mainsail gone.

22.00 What a game! Now squalls up to Force 8. Main down. Burnt my hand trying to mix Smash going to windward at 9 knots. I've got to get north if I'm to stay in one piece.

April 23rd We've gone almost due north all day. I have to get to about 37°S.

I went on deck at 19.00 just to check all was well, going due north on the port tack. I looked at the masthead and nearly had kittens – it was bent well over, the port inner strut was swinging about quite freely. I tacked for the weight to be taken on the starboard shrouds. I'll have to reset it tomorrow – I hope it's not blowing too bad.

Very bad last night, well into Force 8 and gusting 9. I stayed in bed and tried to sleep to blot it out. Mizzen is now ripped in five different places. I'll drop all sail tomorrow, to get up the mast and patch the mizzen.

I'm quite punch-drunk, I'm really worried whether all will be OK for the next 20 or so days.* I keep saying, 'Take your time, and sail only when the weather is right.' That's the trouble – I don't think it ever will be right again until next summer, and each day it gets worse. Although it's only blowing Force 6 now there seems a more vicious side to the wind, as if it was trying to get me before I get round the corner.

I've come 11,384 recorded miles (speedo under-reading?) to windward. That must be the longest wind-ward sail. Yes, I suppose it must be.

April 24th Is it ever going to go down? At 05.30 I was awakened by a bang and the terrific flapping of a sail. I shot out of bed and only just managed to get the mizzen down before I lost it completely. It had blown out. Not at all surprised. I've put up my spare, lovely and brand new. I wonder what Ratsey would say. They recommend it stretched in light winds and I put it up in a 35-knot wind.

Next, the reefing gear jammed. I stripped it as far as I could – it took me 3 hours 15 minutes, mainly spent on getting split pins out. People will insist on bending them right over. It's always the same with people assembling yachting parts; they rarely sail, and don't worry about getting out split pins in 35-knot winds.

_____

* ie, to weather the Cape.

I tried to reset the mast, but no go. It's that inner top shroud again. The masthead is bent like a figure S. So I'm going along under reduced canvas and I feel as frustrated as hell. Still, better safe than sorry. (I suppose.)

Hope to goodness I can get up the mast tomorrow. This is madness, going along like this. I've got to stop pushing and slow down. The devil in me says crash on and take a chance. What a situation to be in!

My last tin of potatoes. Had half with a tin of mince. My, but that's good. New pullover on. Stood for 15 minutes waiting for curry to cook. Thought, 'This is taking a long time.' Hadn't lit the gas.

April 25th At 10.30 I decided to have a go at resetting the mast and got all sail down. I thought it was only the top shrouds which needed tightening – an hour's job. I was wrong. It turned out that the starboard inner shroud needed tightening as well. So out bosun's chair, get changed into loose clothes so I can climb easily. Up the mast, swing out to the end of the crosstree, fix it, come down. Sounds so easy! With a Force 4–5 blowing I was swinging about at the end of the crosstree, even though I'd hooked on. My arms and legs were aching and black and blue, trying to hold on. I very sincerely hope I never have to go up again unless it's calm.

Anyway, I got it straightened, or rather, tightened. I then set up the mast, and now she really is set up well. I feel quite proud. I also set up the mizzen. In for a penny ... Broke my big screwdriver using it as a lever – stupid, but we all do it.

Well, that little lot took me until 17.00 hrs. I then came below and had my last schedule with Perth Radio. The operator seemed quite put out, but I explained about the psychological aspect of speaking to the *advance* station. He appreciated this. Picked up Durban, but no go when I tried to contact them.

April 26th By 11.00 I was becalmed. Never, never would I have thought that I'd be glad to see a calm. This will probably be the only time in my life. I didn't mind it in the least.

I decided it was to be work. Out came the gear to be dried – sleeping bags, pillows, sailing suits, wellingtons, socks, clothes, jumpers, diving suit (still not dried from the last time). Packed away blown-out mizzen. Cleared the forward compartment, and reorganized it. One tomato ketchup and one sandwich spread broken (what a mess and smell). Cleared them up. Then a tin of black-currants leaking. Eventually I sorted it all and repacked. Then lunch. Salmon, potato mayonnaise and French dressing, followed by pears and Nestlé's cream. Had it out in the cockpit. Thought to myself, 'Man, but this sailing is nae sae bad.' (Oh boy, haven't we short memories!)

Stripped off and lay down for half an hour back, half an hour front. It was cold, but the sun was so inviting. Get rid of the bacteria and let the sun recharge me. I felt the skin building up as I lay.

After that it was back to work. Threw away a dozen sardine tins I had from when I sailed to South Africa in 1968. Chris's clock went over the side, rusted up. That was a good clock. Hope Ruth doesn't mind, but it was no good now. I'll have to get them a new one; that one served me well. Three jerry cans over the side. (I can hear Frank saying, 'My drivers are always short.' Sorry, Frank, they are gone now.) Threw away 15 days' D-rations, after getting the goodies from them. I opened them for the tea-bags. I'm almost out of tea-bags and it's going to be a major disaster when they are gone. Last but not least – I threw away my sea anchor. I can hear the old men of the sea and the experts 'Ah, but . . . Ah, but . . .' I've only lain to a sea anchor once in a yacht, and I'd advocate lying

a-hull every time. They aren't worth their weight or space.
I'm only sorry I paid good money for it.

Went into the stern and it smelt to high heaven – bottles
of tonic water broken, about four Guinness cans opened,
and froth all over the place. About three gallons of liquid,
which I can't get out till we move. I think it's fermenting –
I'll have to clear Customs with my own distillery!

April 27th All day the barometer has been dropping.
Copper sky tonight, with all the signs of a gale. My arms
and legs are black and blue still from going up the mast,
and still very sore.

It's now dark, yet before it went dark it was borderline
to dropping the main. I could have dropped it in the
comfort of the light, and I'd have been reasonably OK for
the rest of the night. But now I'm hanging on to it, and I
wonder why? I'm certainly going to have to drop it tonight – why not in comfort instead of groping about
in the dark? I'll have a few more hours at one knot extra
(that's about all the difference it makes in this wind of
30 knots, if indeed it makes any difference). Yet it's
always been the same. Keep her moving. If in doubt, keep
it up.

I'm sorry I can't relax and stop it and so be OK for the
rest of the night. (But start that, and I think it would
expand until I was only sailing in good weather!) There's
my wife and child waiting for me. Maureen's done her
part and did not shirk. Nothing held her up or stopped
her. Now it's my turn to do my part. Keep her moving.
Attack!

20.30 Dropped main. Halyard washed to leeward, got
caught round a cleat, and had to put my hand under the
water as she was heeled over with the cleat under water.
Then it was a climb back up to windward!

April 28th It went calm last night at 02.00, and with a
big sea running *British Steel* was thrown all over the

place. Then it started, shot up to Force 6 again, and it was nothing but heavy rain squalls through the night. Pattern was always the same: came from the north, and as it blew so it would go round the compass, backing until eventually it would go calm, then off we'd go again.

I got into my bunk, dressed, at 05.45 and at 08.30 I was up again, on the tiller again, with more squalls. At 12.30 the wind seemed to settle from the NW at Force 6–7 and I went below and had breakfast – plate of cereal – then very quickly back up to drop the main.

15.00 Very bad squall, which lasted for ages – it covered the whole of the oncoming sky. Dropped No 2 for No 3. It went up to Force 8–9, gusting 10.

Sky cleared just as the sun was due to go down. I lined up the bows on the sun and took a bearing to work out an amplitude in order to check my compass. The result made nonsense of a check I'd made the other day. I'm sure it's my being overtired. I've made a mistake somewhere in the calculation – the calculations are easy, and that's why it's easy to make mistakes. I shall just ignore it, and work on the last completed figures. Besides – one would have to be pretty dull to miss South Africa!

The great fear is, of course, if these calculations are wrong, what of my sights? I think these are OK. Normally it's a reasonable day when I take them, and this helps. Also, I go over them very carefully.

Went to bed at 19.30 and woke at 21.00, with the wind down to Force 4. I knew that I must get up to set the main. I was slow getting up – the trip is definitely slowing. The effect now is that I lie and ask myself 'You could lie a-hull – what's a few more extra days?' But always the same thought comes, 'You're not out here for a holiday. What would Maureen and Samantha say?'

As I begin to get my suit on I promise myself a nice tin of chicken soup, or a whisky, or a Guinness, always some wee bonus. Seldom do I get any of them – I've forgotten all about it by the time I get below again.

During a squall I was bracing myself while on the tiller, using my leg pressing against the mizzen. I slipped off, shot forward and banged my head. Not to worry, there was no damage to the mizzen.

April 29th 12.00 Right this minute, it's blowing over 60 knots. I'm lying a-hull. I'm so shattered, it's dangerous.

At 08.00 I dropped the main. Barometer 995 by 10.30. Now, at 12.00, 989, and dropping. Waves breaking right over us.

When I was dropping the No 2 little circles came flooding in front of me – a warning I was exhausted. I had eaten hardly anything yesterday, and so far nothing today. I never thought I'd see the day when I was off my food due to exhaustion. I went below and rammed (not ate) two Mars bars down me. Got all the sails securely lashed, except the boomed foresail which I left up.

12.20 Boomed foresail halyard parted. Now no sail up. Wind speedo reading over 60 knots – off scale. Waves enormous, and getting bigger. Keep getting thrown on our side to about 50 deg. Now you know why I wanted steel! I must eat, I must.

13.00 Barometer 987. Please God let the storm go down.

14.00 Barometer 986. When is it going to stop? The wind is well over 60 knots, that's Force 12.

I've checked the bow and stern, and pumped out. Very little water, that's the beauty of a steel yacht. I've checked the watertight doors, and secured. I must consider running under bare poles, but I don't want to.

Had a tin of mince and carrots. Will lie down and try to sleep. But how the hell can you sleep getting hurled about like this, and with the noise? Every now and again we take a big one, then there's a loud bang.

I've 1,210 miles to go to 30°E.* Once there I'll be OK I'm sure. I just have to survive this one, and I'll be reasonably OK. Surely I can't have one as bad as this within the next two weeks? I doubt if I can stand it.

My arms and legs ache. All this fatigue is not from this one storm, it's a cumulation of the voyage from the Horn. The continual struggle to get west, the heeling over, the banging, the crashing against the waves, no self-steering gear. Always having to move on, sail-changing. This is what has has been rubbing away at me, gently, but each a little harder than yesterday.

I have two weeks, just two weeks to go,† and I should be OK, please God. Soon it will be a memory.

Stop whining and moaning. This is what it's all about. Not the sun, not the pleasant days, but this – a survival environment.

14.15 Heavy rain squall. Good. The rain will break the seas down a little bit.

Everywhere is white, spray gets knocked off the waves with such ferocity. I was going to try and take a photograph, but it's ludicrous.

The Atlantic was never like this. The waves follow one after the other like legions going into battle. The discipline is rigid, as one wave goes down, another rises to take its place.

If I ever dream, I'll dream of this storm. The hurricanes in the Atlantic never haunted me, but this one could. I just close my eyes and see those white-blue legions rising and falling, but always advancing.

My heart goes out to the men at Dartmouth at Philip's yard. It would only have taken one of them to have shirked his job, and the sea would find the weak spot, and

* The longitude of South Africa between Durban and East London which I set as a kind of target for this leg of the voyage.
† ie, to 30°E.

then it would work on it until it got us. Stay strong, *British Steel*. You have my life in your hands now. There is nothing I can do. It's up to you, and our Lord.

First time in my life I've been honestly and genuinely frightened. It's always been a kind of curiosity. But here now I'll say, without any embarrassment, I am frightened.

15.00 Heavy rain again. Sheets and sheets of it, straight down. It's knocked the seas down a bit. Wind had dropped to 40 knots. I think we're going to be OK. I'm going to bed now to get a sleep (or at least try). Ready for the next bout.

17.30 Barometer 986. Still blowing 40–60 knots, plus rain squalls. Had a wee sleep. Feel like death, but up.

Saw sun go down, or part of it. Copper-coloured, indicating bad weather will continue. I would like something to eat, but don't know what. Put the tape recorder on loud to drown the noise. Peculiar noise coming from the rudder – hope it's OK.

18.00 Wind dropped. Made a great fetish of closing everything up and then eating. Had chicken soup (spilt) then potato salad and salmon. Had to force it down. Now I don't feel so hot, but I know it will help.

20.30 Barometer 987. Wind has dropped a little. The worst part is that I'll have been pushed east, both by the current and the wind, and now I'll have to re-sail those miles. If I'd been going the other way I'd have been able to run smack east, and really logged the miles. It breaks my heart.

22.00 It's up again, 55 knots. I'm having a Guinness and going to bed. I pray it's all over soon. It would be sensible to turn and run, but I'd rather take the punishment of being thrown about than go east.

April 30th, 12.30 I slept – man, but I slept! Got up at 10.30. Barometer 998, wind Force 8–9 from the SW. At

12.00 I thought I'd go and get the No 3 ready, and worked out how I was going to get the boomed foresail up with her having a broken halyard. I'm going to use the boom topping lift until I can get up the mast. Not ideal, but better than nothing, and I think it will be strong enough.

Well, by 12.30 I was ready to go, and then a squall, sending the wind speedo back to 55 knots. It's black now, and I have to use the light. I don't mean *dark*, I mean *black*. This is a bad storm. It's now been over twenty-four hours. The seas are ludicrous – surely they can't get any bigger? I'm getting those funny things in front of my eyes again, though I've had some porridge this morning. I'm beginning to think they are caused by fear.

15.30 Barometer 1001, but still blowing 40–50 knots. Sun out, I took some photographs – some pantomime leaping in and out, trying to keep the camera dry.

Doubtful if I'll sail now until tomorrow – that will mean forty-eight hours lying a-hull. I should think we have been pushed back over 100 miles.

Still had nothing to eat since my porridge. Better try and choke something down.

17.30 Barometer 1003, but it's still blowing. Is it ever going to stop? I think it will be down by tomorrow morning – I hope so, anyway.

22.30 Now it's Force 6. Barometer 1009. I could sail, but I'm not. I'll give it a chance to get right away, there's still the odd squall blowing. Two days lost, and it will take me another day to regain the miles that we've been pushed back.

Those log entries, written hurriedly at intervals of being hurled across the cabin or clinging on for dear life, convey better than any words I can find now the reality of that storm. I cannot pretend that they convey it well – I think no one can come near to meaningful description of such an experience. The words we have to use – 'gigantic', 'fear', 'banging and crashing', for instance – have all been devalued by the way we use them in everyday life. The *enormity* of a storm at sea is so far removed from normal experience that I can ask the reader only to try to read between the words, to understand that the reality was infinitely more horrifying than anything the words suggest.

The storm left me feeling drained and shaken. It also left me a number of practical problems, which I had to force myself to tackle. Chief among these was that *all* my jib halyards had parted, so that I could set no headsails. And without headsails the yacht could not be expected to sail properly. On May 1st the storm moderated, but the wind was still at Gale Force 8, and without a jib I reckoned that we could make no more than about 4 knots. And as the yacht was constantly being stopped by heavy seas, our effective speed was probably about 1 knot.

That would not do. I managed to set my storm jib using the boom topping lift for a halyard. It was better than nothing, but I feared that it would not stand up long in strong winds. So I *had* to get up the mast. I prayed for a calm, and on Sunday morning, May 2nd, I reckoned that it was just about calm enough to tackle the job. After two cups of coffee and my last tin of kippers I went up, with the tail lines for halyards attached to me. I had a fearful job to hang on – and discovered how useful teeth are! As I needed both hands for most of the time to hang on I held the line in my teeth.

My first job was to thread the line through the spare central sheave, and once that was done there was the same procedure to be gone through for the jib-block. Then I had to cut the old halyard (wire galvanized), which had parted. I managed this using wire-cutters. It was no joke hanging on swaying, and trying to cut wire, but I succeeded at the cost

of the wire-cutters, which broke their spring. Next I poured
a whole tube of lubricant over the main halyard sheave,
which had been sticking.

I got as far as the jumper-struts, pulling the tail for the jib
halyard behind me, when I saw the light line I used for
threading the central sheave rising, and about to run out. I
nearly cried. Holding on with one hand and jamming myself
in among the jumpers I grabbed for the line, missed it a few
times, and finally caught it with just about a yard left to
run.

Then I had to pass the halyards through the jumpers and
the rest of the rigging so that they wouldn't chafe. I got a bit
tangled up, couldn't decide what went where, and so had to
come down. I sorted out the halyards on deck and had to go
up again as far as the jumper struts to make sure that they
had a clear run.

Then lunch – pears and evaporated milk. Over lunch I
decided that I'd change the mizzen halyard as well, to have a
new one *before* the old one broke! I'd never been up the
mizzen mast before, and although it is twenty feet shorter
than the main, I didn't like the look of it – it seemed awfully
bare. Actually, it turned out to be easy to climb, with the
shrouds just the right distance apart for comfortable going.
Also, the mizzen is not so wide as the mainmast, and that
helped.

I ended up with a new jib halyard (single purchase), a new
boomed-foresail halyard, a nearly new main halyard, well
soaked in Seawife wax, and a new mizzen halyard, also well
coated in wax. This was messy stuff to put on, but well worth
it.

I was pleased with the work, though it cost me a bad
bruise on my right arm. I was less pleased with a sight I got
which showed that I'd been blown back 160 miles to the
south-east by the storm.

That evening there was not a cloud in the sky, but the

wind was blowing at 35 knots. I didn't feel like food, but forced myself to eat three cream crackers spread with sandwich spread. My urine was very dark, and I feared that I was getting a bit dehydrated. I told myself that I must drink more.

Monday, May 3rd was calm all day. It was hard to believe that the sea was capable of being so vicious. The sun shone, and I had another day of maintenance, patching the mainsail and putting anti-chafe round all the halyards. I also put a long overdue charge into the batteries.

On Tuesday the barometer began dropping again, falling from 1003 at 10.00 hours to 992 at 18.00. I expected high winds, but with the exception of one 40-knot squall the wind didn't go above Force 7. The great event of this day was that I managed to get *British Steel* to run by herself for a bit. It was not too good, but an encouraging prospect for the trade winds, when (if ever) I got to them. I busied my mind trying to work out whether there was any way of mending my broken running booms. It might, I thought, be just possible.

There was no chance, however, of tackling the booms then, for the pattern of squalls and heavy weather returned. My log notes:

May 5th Nasty squall last night, up to 45 knots. I lay in bed looking at the wind speedo and willed it to go away. My logic was that by the time I got dressed and on deck, it would be gone. After 10 minutes it was obvious that I'd have to get up. I crawled forward to drop the main, water rushing past right up to my knees.

21.15 We've just been hit by an enormous wave, smack on the bow, straight over us, filling the cockpit and pouring in through the doorway. We stopped dead. If we hadn't had water pouring over us I'd have said that we'd hit a whale (or a ship).

May 6th I'm absolutely fed up with this place, it reall
is wearing me down. I'm having to draw strength from
Maureen to keep going. How long can I last like this?

Woke at 06.30 (pitch black) to the No 3 (foresail) bang
ing madly. Dressed, went on deck, and a flash of the torc
showed that the forestay had parted. My heart sank. I
turned out not so bad – the toggle on the bottle-screw ha
parted. Dropped the sail and lay a-hull till dawn. Back o
deck at dawn, and an hour later we were on our way. Ha
to take off all the Ramsey hanks and it was a bore. Also
when I went to get a spare toggle, the drawer jammed.
split it open with a hammer and screwdriver. Now n
drawer.

Went into the cockpit to winch in the No 3 withou
putting suit on. No good, big dollop on my back. Tore m
shirt off in a fit of temper and threw it overboard
Definitely a bad sign.

Received two radio messages, one from Frank [Allen
and one from the Senior British Naval Officer in South
Africa wishing me luck for the remainder of th
voyage.

22.30 We've just been hit by I don't know what. Wind
is now Force 8–9. We got hit with one big one, stopped u
dead, and then its buddy came along for good measure
Normally the worst one is the first, here it was reversed
Luckily I was lashed into the galley. Plates flew out o
their special place, packet of biscuits went spilling out
leaving a mess everywhere. Jar of Marmite fell, but luck
ily didn't break. One plate did break (and they are almos
unbreakable). Worse to come – an opened packet of milk
So we got milk on the chart table, on the radio, every
where. Worse still, the chip pan, full, oil everywhere. A lo
of oil went in my supper (tin of mince). I thought, to hel
with it, and ate very oily mince. I've never been sick at sea
but nearly after this lot . . .

May 7th 60-knot squall. During breakfast I spilt the coffee container on the floor, and as the floor was wet, it all stuck to it. Boiled some water and washed it away – coffee stains everywhere.

Not feeling so hot after last night's oily mixture, and have hardly eaten anything all day. Will try tonight.

19.00 (*approx*) Tummy not too good still. I got out my only packet of Ritz crackers. I'd been saving them for a special occasion, this was it. But they were soaked, just soggy damp. Nothing to do but toss them away. A bad blow.

Midnight At about 20.00 she swung to the SW, so I went to tack. This meant dropping No 3 and mizzen. First mizzen, so I could get the bow away from the waves and run off. As soon as that was done I ran forward and dropped the No 3. With the tiller to one side she doesn't run east, but just lies a-hull with the boomed foresail up. (Not technically a heave-to.) It only takes a couple of minutes to do that lot (I've had a little practice!). Well, I'd these two just down and I felt the wind increasing. I looked forward, spray biting into me, my eyes screwed up to peer into the night. There, just on the horizon, it was like a white sandy beach. I just stood and stared. I couldn't understand what it was. Then it clicked. I turned, dropped the boomed foresail and had just got it down when it hit us. What a squall! (Lasted about an hour.)

I clawed my way to the cockpit, looked at the wind speedo and it was off the scale. It could have been 70 or even 90 knots at one time.

Down below fast – length of line to cut more (sail) ties. I've a very sharp knife in the galley drawer. Tried to pull it out, but the drawer was jammed. I yanked the handle – pulled it off. I cursed, used my own knife, and cut ties to further secure the already lashed down sails. Lay a-hull till 21.30. Then Force 8, so off we go again, a little more frightened, a little more worried.

May 8th, 09.30 It's force 8 from the W. I really am worried. I just cannot see how we are to beat round the Cape with these conditions. You may say, Lie a-hull when it's bad. But that only means I'll be pushed back. I keep saying, Take it steady, relax, don't go so hard, plenty of time. But I can't, I just can't. Even last night, with all the sails lashed down, when the wind dropped to Force 8, I was off. I've got to keep going. My great fear is the mast. If that goes, I have no chance of getting round, none at all. I'm praying very hard for our Lord's assistance. It will be Him that gets us out of here and round the Cape.

Last night, as I flew downstairs to get the extra ties, I tripped on a container, which is normally beside the steps, jammed in. This holds cameras, films, etc. I picked it up and quickly jammed it in its place. After getting the ties I ran to get on deck. The container was in the way again. I cursed, and gave it one almighty kick. I thought I'd broken my foot. It's still aching now. Serves me right.

That evening I was delighted to raise Port Elizabeth on the radio. I'd just finished sending a couple of telegrams when I looked over the stern and saw the lights of a ship coming straight at me. I switched on my navigation lights and got all my emergency gear ready, Aldis lamp, flares, etc. I tried to start the engine, but it wouldn't respond.

I flashed my Aldis lamp at the ship, but there was no answer. It just came straight on. I thought, 'Right, I'll wake up the officer on watch.' So I got one of my explosives, lit it, counted nine (they have a 14-second fuse), and threw it high into the air. There was a bang and a blinding flash – that woke them up all right. The ship lit up like Blackpool illuminations. I then challenged with the Aldis lamp again,

and within a few seconds a reply came. I couldn't make head
or tail of it.

By this time the ship had stopped, and was now abeam of
me. I tried my engine again, but it still wouldn't work. My
starboard light then fused, so to let him know where I was, I
kept my port light to him, which meant going downwind of
him. I passed about 100 yards away and yelled, 'Radio-telephone 2182' (the international calling frequency). I got no
answer, so I tacked and went to his stern, closing to about
twenty yards, but I was now upwind of him, so I was OK.
There were about thirty blokes all lined along the deck. I
yelled half a dozen times, and then, after what seemed an
age, somebody said 'OK radio 2182.' I sailed off and hove
to, and got on my radio set.

Sure enough, he came up on the radio. We changed to
working frequencies (2182, although the calling frequency,
is reserved, in use, for distress calls). I said, 'OK, please
continue your journey, and I'll talk to you on the phone.' It
turned out that he was a Russian fishing vessel called *Zare-
chensk* and we had quite a yarn. He gave me my position,
and I apologized for making him stop. He said that was no
matter. I then explained about my circumnavigation, and he
wished me luck. I told him that I'd met Mr Kosygin in
London. I don't think he believed this, but he said, 'Congratulations to your Queen.' He then said that he had to
make a rendezvous with another fishing vessel, and we said
goodbye. He was a big boat, and I think perhaps he was a
factory ship for the fishing fleet.

I went to bed feeling much happier after this meeting, but
a bit cross with myself for having forgotten to ask him to
report me to Lloyds.

CHAPTER EIGHT

Round the Corner

May 14th was my thirty-first birthday. I got up at 07.00 and opened my special pack – birthday cards from Maureen, Samantha, Maureen's mother, my sister, the Allens and the Waddingtons. From Clare Allen a letter saying 'If this trip doesn't satisfy you, try one of these' – and enclosing a P & O brochure! My presents included a pair of scarlet slippers and (also from Maureen) *The Cruel Sea* (great sense of humour). For goodies – my favourite Highland toffee, ham, chicken, rice, and all the ingredients (even garlic) to make my favourite Indonesian dish of Nasigorin. There were lots of other good things, and a little note from Maureen saying 'Sorry, no lettuce.' I marvelled again at Maureen's care for detail, and felt (for the ten thousandth time) how lucky I was in my wife.

I had the ham for lunch and then opened a packet of brandy snaps and a tin of Nestlé's cream. Saying to myself, 'If I don't eat them now they will get damp,' I polished off the lot: what an excuse! But how I enjoyed them!

As a further treat I had a shave, getting rid of the longest beard I've ever had. It was awful, and a joy to get rid of it.

Perhaps my best birthday present, however, was to pass longitude 30°E, the invisible line that had been my target for what seemed months. I was not round the corner yet, and had another 10 degrees to reach Cape Agulhas at longitude 20° E, but I felt that at last I could really feel that I had reached South African waters.

Since my meeting with the Russian ship on May 9th I had spent most of my time working on the engine, to try to get it to go. I didn't need it for motive power (though it was there for emergencies) but I did need it for charging my all-important batteries. I changed a solenoid and got the engine running for about an hour, when I noticed smoke coming from the regulator. So I switched off, and after that nothing I could do would make it start.

I wasn't all that worried because I had the little Honda charging-motor as a standby, and I got some charge into the batteries with that. But there was something wrong with the ammeter. It began flickering and reading wildly, and finally, although the engine ran, I could get no charge out of it at all. I studied the Honda manual and decided that it needed an ammeter replacement – and I had no spare.

This was serious, for without being able to charge the batteries I could have no radio, instruments (wind speed indicator, etc) cabin lights, navigation lights or electric bilge pump. But I did have paraffin lamps and candles, so I could get by. There was enough charge in the batteries to keep the radio going for a bit if I used it sparingly. I sent a telegram to Frank Allen, who had been on an instruction course with me at the Perkins engine factory, asking if he could get me advice about the engine, and I stopped using the batteries for lighting, or anything other than the radio and instruments.

The weather continued much as it had been, with fierce squalls interspersed with an occasional spell of calm. On the day after my birthday we had another storm, with winds of well over 60 knots. The waves this time were shorter than before, but wickedly sharp, due, I think to the Agulhas current, which runs off the coast of South Africa, meeting the wind over tide. We lay a-hull, heeling over about 60 degrees.

I sat jammed to the chart table and just hung on. Somehow I was much less frightened than before; what we had come through already had given me ultimate confidence in *British Steel*.

On May 16th the weather moderated. The storm left me with a broken tiller, but I was able to fix up a jury tiller, using the shaft of the vane from the now useless self-steering gear. I wrote up my log by candlelight. I had twelve candles, and I reckoned that I could get by on half a candle a night. That would give me candlelight for twenty-four nights, and I still had five gallons of paraffin.

The P & O liner *Oronsay* was in the vicinity, with my friend Bruce Maxwell on board. Bruce had some letters for me, and I'd hoped that we might be able to meet at sea, but this turned out to be impracticable because of our relative positions. But I was able to get in touch with the *Oronsay* by radio, and her radio-operator was most helpful in relaying messages from me to save my batteries. Cape Town Radio also helped by transmitting messages for me 'blind' – ie without waiting for me to make a contact with them. That meant that I had simply to tune in and listen, using far less current than if I had had to call up and transmit.

After the lull on May 16th the weather worsened again, and I went through one of the most unnerving moments of the whole voyage. I was at the tiller and a big wave crept up on me. I didn't see it until the last moment, when it broke right over us – only about one in a million waves hit like this. The whole deck, cockpit, everywhere was covered in water, and save for the mast and rigging we were completely submerged. I just sat, holding the tiller, and steering *under* water, as if I were steering a submarine. For a split second I wondered if we were going to come up – but up *British Steel* rose again, and all was well.

I was now in the shipping lanes again, which meant that I couldn't turn in after dark, but had to stay on watch. My eyes were sore with spray, and I had to bathe them frequently with fresh water to keep them open.

On May 20th I was close to weathering Cape Agulhas, but the wind stayed in the west and headed me. Then it fell away altogether and we were becalmed. My log notes irritably:

May 20th We've had two storms in four days, and now when we're almost round the corner, I'm becalmed. Becalmed right in the middle of the shipping lanes, with no lights. It's like Piccadilly Circus outside. I've just counted seven ships and one fishing boat.

One of the ships I saw was a supertanker; all I saw was her bridge and her bow wave seemingly miles ahead – I couldn't see her deck at all. Such great ships terrified me. I didn't expect them to alter course for me, but I did pray that somebody on board was keeping a proper watch, to signal with Aldis lamp or fog horn if it seemed that they were going to pass me close. I kept the sails up even though there was no wind, so that I could at least show some white.

Early in the morning of May 21st I had a close shave. My log describes it.

May 21st 01.45 I'm shaking like a bloody leaf. I just can't control it. We've been close to being run down before, but never as close as this. When he veered off, he must have been less than fifty yards away. I flew for the life-raft. I had my emergency lights. I flashed my light – still he came on. Fog horn – no use when he's got a diesel in his ear. I got him with an explosive, not a second too soon. He must have been half-asleep – he heeled over like billy as he sheered off. I can't write what I called out. I tried to get the ship's name, but after running for the life-raft I was a bit too late.

After that dreadful night my last log entry for May 21st was a triumph. It reads:

Sent telegram to Maureen. 34° 50′S, 19° 20′E. Turned right 15.00 GMT. We are on our way north. Hullo Atlantic – goodbye Indian Ocean.

I was due for a rendezvous off the Cape, and at dawn on May 22nd I dropped all sails and radioed my position to Cape Town. I was about seventeen miles offshore. There was nothing to do but wait, so I thought I might as well turn in. The next thing I heard was a voice amplified through a loudspeaker. I looked out, and there was a ship of the South African Navy. I hailed them to wait and not to come alongside until I was ready because of my paintwork. I changed quickly into clean clothes and went up to signal them in. Petty Officer Kruger brought a boat alongside and gave me a telex from Maureen, a parcel from the British Ambassador in South Africa and a pile of magazines. I spoke to the skipper (Lt-Commander Nick Smitt) by radio and thanked him. I yarned with my boatload of visitors, who included Mr Young of Yorkshire TV for about three quarters of an hour and we all had a couple of Guinnesses. Then they left.

When they'd gone I debated whether to opt for another sleep, or work. I decided on work, and set about repairing one of the running poles by fitting a sleeve to it. That took all afternoon, but it gave me one pole ready for use (at least, unless it decided to break again) and I had hopes of being able to repair the other.

The British Ambassador's parcel contained two bottles of champagne and a jar of caviar. I sent him a telegram of thanks, and said that I'd keep one bottle to share with Maureen when I got home, and have the other when I recrossed my outward track and so completed my circumnavigation. I was able to make a radio-telephone call to Maureen, and it was great to hear her. She seemed much better than when we had last spoken, and said that she was keeping well. That cheered me up and encouraged me enormously.

I don't quite know what I *really* expected on turning north after weathering the Cape, 'turning the corner', as I used to say to myself. I think half of me expected to meet trade winds, warm sun and mermaids almost at once. Of course it didn't turn out like that. I found myself beating and slogging just as before. I kept shouting to myself, 'Hey, what's the deal? I'm supposed to be running. What's all this waves and spray? Where are the mermaids, the flying fish and the iced Pepsi?' But my spirits stayed high. I told myself, 'Not to worry. It will come.'

I tackled the Honda again, and managed to fix it. There were two wires loose which needed soldering. I'd never soldered anything in my life before, but I did have a soldering iron and some solder on board. They were sent to me as a gift by someone who had read Robin Knox-Johnston's book and remembered Robin's need of a soldering iron. Lord, I was grateful! I didn't want to make a mistake, so I called up Cape Town Radio and asked for instructions on soldering; and received most practical and helpful instructions from the operator, George Allen. All went well, and as soon as the job was done I got the machine running and put a charge in the batteries.

My log for this period becomes much more cheerful.

May 24th Had a visitor at approx 14.00 MV *Miapura* from Liverpool. When I saw him coming across I got out the Red Ensign and hoisted. Blow me, if he didn't do the same! It was very thrilling, in this obscure part of the sea, to see two Red Ensigns.

Got my sails organized for the run home. That took a lot of work, moving all the gear. I've now 10 sails on deck.

May 25th Met the BP tanker *British Sailor*. Sounded odd calling him up, '*British Steel* for *British Sailor*.' He stopped, and I sailed across to him. They came from La Plata to Cape Town. Thanked them for stopping.

I began to pick up the southerly winds I'd been longing for, but I still had the greatest difficulty in getting the yacht to run by herself. I had no luck with the mended running pole; when I put it up it lasted barely three hours before it broke again. I repaired it again, and again it broke. This time I had a lot of trouble in getting the broken pole down, for it got tangled up with the running sail. As soon as it was down I had yet another go at repairing it, cutting out the broken part to make a new fit for the sleeve. It was a horrible job, for all the rivets had to be drilled out. My fingers developed blisters from the drilling and I cut my hand, but I restored the pole, though its length was now reduced from 25 to 19 feet. Then I tackled the other broken pole. The only metal sleeve I had was really too big, but I clamped it round the boom and held it with my portable vice until I got the rivets to hold. I wasn't all that pleased with the repairs, but by June 1st was able to get both poles up and to get *British Steel* running more or less successfully on her own. It was not wholly successful, because with the poles of unequal length she tended to pull off course to one side. But I corrected this to some extent by fitting shock-cord to the tiller, and by fiddling with the sheets of the running sails. These not wholly satisfactory arrangements were vastly better than nothing, for they enabled me to leave the yacht to herself from time to time while I got some sleep or cooked a meal. Until I could get her to run by herself I couldn't safely leave the tiller even for five minutes – I had to steer even while using the lavatory bucket.

I told myself that I mustn't be cross about all my troubles with the poles. They were not strong enough, and that was that. It was a mistake, and anyone can make a mistake. When I felt myself wanting to curse the people responsible for the poles, I asked myself, 'What about the mast?' That had taken a terrific hammering, and was still up. So I would say to myself, 'Which would you rather have, mast or poles?' That made me see things in a truer perspective.

A long talk on the radio telephone with Frank Allen enabled me to fix the engine. We went over the starting problem piece by piece – Frank knew every detail of the installation and the circuits – and with his help I was able to trace the fault and put it right. It was an immense relief to know that I could charge the batteries from the engine again, and to be able once more to afford electric light.

Some jottings from my log:

June 3rd Today I feel utterly contented with my lot in life. Few times do I ever feel it, but today was one of them. It's a very pleasant feeling, sheer bliss; I couldn't have worried today had a submarine come up underneath me.

Listened to the BBC (World Service) News for the first time for a long time. If anything is designed to depress you, that is. They must *look* for all the Nitty Gritty. Death, blood, murders, drownings – nothing, but *nothing* on a light note. I doubt if I will listen to it again, but I will listen to the other programmes.

Changed charts – it really is great to be sorting out my next set of charts, which take me up to the Azores.

June 4th The wind is from the east, and I'm writing this while altering the tiller every now and again. This is a real drag, only being able to get her to run when the wind is directly astern. At present I've the ghosting Genoa up, with No 1 foresail boomed out to starboard, and the mizzen up, the latter for balance. It looks squally, so I'm not putting the mizzen staysail up tonight. It's going to be all night on the tiller. It's *almost* balanced, but not quite. I could leave it for 10–20 minutes, but certainly no longer.

June 5th Jobs to do:

    Boomed-foresail halyard

    Main halyard

    No 1 halyard (re-sleeve, double purchase)

    Repair emergency lights

    Finish sewing No 2 (foresail)

    Sew No 1

    Repair pump (cockpit)

    Repair stowage bins

    Repair locker door

    Organize and clear stern

    Organize forward sail bins

    Arrange books

    Clean dressing on finger

    Rust off mast

    Clean and lubricate winches

    Paint deck

    Wash and shave

These are the most immediate. I've dozens more, like the stove really needs cleaning. I'm damned if I'm going back with a 'gungy' yacht!

(*Later*) I've done one or two jobs since I wrote the list. Boomed-foresail up – that's the halyard that had parted. Repaired starboard lamp by stealing from the port – I've got two port emergency lights, so that's OK. Got the main halyard ready and greased, using *Seawife*. That's a messy job, but certainly worth it as far as galvanized halyards are concerned. In harbour, I'd get Samantha to do it. She'd love it!

June 6th A great sadness, saw a dead bird. It looked like an Arctic tern. It couldn't have been dead long, it still looked in reasonable shape. Wonder how on earth it died here.

My first tin of bad food. I'll have to be careful now, I'd hate to get food poisoning at this stage.

Went calm for a few hours, so I sheeted sails hard and went to sleep.

June 7th Woke from my few hours' sleep to a dark sky and squalls every so often. Going along with No 1 main and boomed-foresail. When a squall comes, I just turn and go before it. I've had wind from the east now for a few days. Great nuisance. If it was from the SE I could go under running sail.

Have gone all native again. Towel over my head (very stylish), sunglasses, and trousers rolled up.

I kicked my foot against one of the cleats by the cockpit. Oh boy, is it sore! It's swollen, now, as well.

Wrote this (and yesterday) while on the tiller.

June 8th It's 13.15 hrs and I'm on the tiller (as usual). I'm desperately trying to keep awake.

No success at running, so it's heave-to for a sleep.

(*Later*) The frustration caused by not getting her to hold a course is having an effect on me. She balances like a dream, but the minute the wind alters, off she goes. My back is absolutely aching.

Goodness me, my logs must read awfully, whining on like some old goat. There isn't a problem, really. To sit and steer in the sun is great – people all over the earth enjoy the pleasure. It's just that I have this attitude – I must get home as soon as possible. I cannot shake it off, no matter how many arguments I give myself for taking it easy and just getting home eventually. We've covered 100 miles a day since picking up the SE Trades, but really not good enough. I'm getting 120-110-115-122 miles a day, when it should be 150/180. But I can't stay awake all the time.

Learning poetry while on the tiller. In four days I learnt

six poems off pat, and now I'm getting Burns mixed up
with Masefield.

June 9th I was very disappointed with today's astro
position – exactly 90 miles due south of St Helena. This
means I went quite far to the SW last night. It swung to
the NE, and she went off to swing SW. It's been Force 1
(if you could call it that) from the NE all day.

It boils down to this: (1) Can't get her to hold a course
while I sleep when running, (2) Can't get full spread of
sail due to short booms, (3) Light winds and running – her
worst point of sailing, (4) Very badly fouled hull, (5) I'm
tired, and enthusiasm creeps from me daily.

Anyway, I've decided to enjoy the sail back and not to
worry about the time. This is the greatest adventure I'll
ever be on, and now is the time when it should be enjoyed
and thought over. It was hard work (and frightening)
from Horn to Cape, and this should be a time for recuper-
ating.

As a start, I had for lunch sardines, followed by raspberries and Nestlé's cream, coffee and Drambuie. I've
found two dozen mandarin oranges (tins). One of Maureen's favourites.

Also had a shave and a bath. Feeling a lot better for it.
Strutting about the deck with only towel over my head
(what style!) and a pair of sunglasses. Only like this for 1½
hours till I build up against the sun, although I seldom
burn or peel – better safe than sorry.

Also found a bottle of TCP. This is good news, I'd
only half a bottle left. Means I can have it in my weekly
washes again.

June 10th Well, we've made St Helena, but only just. I
got up after being becalmed last night, and there it was on
the bow, approx 30–40 miles away. Amazing this astro
navigation. I say land tomorrow, and *expect* it.

Got contact with Cape Town. He had a telegram from

Hawick for me. I was thrilled at getting it, the more so this weekend because of the Common Riding – Hawick's Annual Festival. My blue and yellow will be flying and I'll be hoarse with singing. Only a Tern knows the fever of this weekend. I'm with you in spirit, Hawick.

18.00 St Helena is still about 5–10 miles north of me. Didn't think I'd ever see St Helena again. Last time I had my crew – what a wonderful trip that was with Maureen. I have been very fortunate with my life. Wonderfully happy family. Great time as a child. High-school days and swimming will always be deeply cherished. Great times and comrades in the Paras. Eight years of contented and happy marriage. Samantha, whom I worship. And this trip. What next? Can my life get any better? Or am I near the apex? Happiness and love has abounded.

saw the first flying fish of the return voyage off St Helena – hat really was a sign of getting on. But we were getting on o slowly in those light airs that we seemed to be making carcely any progress. I resigned myself to being at sea until he end of August. To keep my mind off such thoughts I lecided to tackle a really dirty job – cleaning out and tidying up the stern. I began by throwing away nine bottles of wine which seemed to have become travel-sick. I hoped that the champagne, of which I had four bottles, didn't go like that. After a good spell of housework in the stern lockers I opened my last tin of ham to celebrate getting past St Helena. I had to admit that I wasn't yet quite past the island but I reckoned that it was close enough to count.

A radio message from Phil Wolfinden told me that there were some Royal Navy ships in the area, and that they might ry to contact me. Next day I tried to get in touch with them. But I didn't know the names of the ships and it seemed silly o go on the air with '*British Steel* calling HMS *Blank*.' nstead, I called up St Helena Radio and, at the fourth try, got a reply, 'St Helena Radio for *British Steel*.' I explained to the operator that I didn't really want St Helena Radio but was trying to call the Navy. Fortunately he saw the funny side of this, and we had a good yarn. He told me that the naval units were HMS *Eagle* and HMS *Glamorgan* and that they had left Ascension yesterday. They were still on exercise, and it was doubtful if I would see them without first making radio contact. Since I'd no idea in which direction they'd gone, this seemed unlikely. It was a pity. If only I'd been a few days earlier I'd almost certainly have met them.

The operator also told me that not long ago a yacht arrived from South Africa and the crew of four went ashore for a few drinks. When they went back to their yacht it had gone. It had been stolen, and had just turned up at Recife in South America. It was lucky, I thought that the thief hadn't felt like stealing yachts the night Maureen and I stayed ashore when we put in at St Helena.

As night fell I wondered if naval ships carried lights when they were on exercise. I should have hated to bump into an aircraft carrier!

Once past St Helena I picked up some wind, and in 24 hours from June 11th–12th I logged 150 miles. It was grand sailing, in warm sunshine. I stayed at the tiller all day, and carried on all through the night. That helped me to cover the miles, but my back and backside got wretchedly sore. Two birds of a sort I'd never seen before flew round us during the day. The first was white, with black markings on its wings and a very sharp pointed beak. The second was white, with long slim tail and a red beak. He flew round and round *British Steel* but at last decided against landing and made off, heading north-east. I pointed to the direction of St Helena, but he ignored me.

Another good day's run of 150 miles saw me halfway towards Ascension Island. To put in the maximum amount f time at the tiller with the minimum of sleep I revised my working hours. I stayed up until 02.00, then went to bed and lept until dawn – the dawn always woke me. Then back to he tiller. If I went to bed at 22.00 hrs I'd almost certainly leep through the night.

After much more experimenting I was at last getting the 'acht to sail herself with the wind on her quarter, but only at bout 3–4 knots. That wasn't exactly satisfying but at least it neant that we could keep going in the right direction while I ,ot some sleep.

I found continual sitting at the tiller both physically tiring nd mentally rather bemusing. I suppose that after a time it had a sort of hypnotic effect. I kept thinking that I'd written hings in the log when in fact I hadn't. I tried reading at the iller, but it was no good – I'd find myself reading the same aragraph a dozen times over. Pictures would have been etter – I felt that I should have equipped myself with piles f comics! Puzzles were useful, the sort where you have to letach rings, or put odd shapes together to make squares.

On June 15th I was at 8° 40′S, 11° 30′W. I came up to ind my first flying fish on deck, dead. I hate finding them ike this. If I'd heard him flop down on deck I'd have got up nd thrown him back into the sea. But I slept through the ittle noise he made on coming aboard.

It was getting very warm in the cockpit now, and down 'elow I took to sleeping on top of my sleeping bag instead f in it. I gave myself another haircut, real Yul Brynner 'tyle! I reckoned that it would have a chance to grow a bit 'efore I got back.

I read up Robin Knox-Johnston's book about how he lealt with barnacles. He was quite successful in getting them ff, but I couldn't manage to do much with mine. From the lescription I was sure that both his barnacles and mine were he same type. I wondered if the apparently greater sticking 'owers of mine were anything to do with the paint, or with the difference between a steel and a wooden hull.

My log again:

June 16th I've been on the tiller all night. Reason: light winds, so carried maximum sail. At 06.00 I thought I had a schedule with Cape Town. I couldn't pick them up, and they didn't hear my calls. It may have been for 07.00. I wasn't too sure, but thought it was 06.00. The wind got up a little to Force 3-4, and I dropped the ghoster and waited for 07.00. My back was aching, so I decided to lie on my back and steer.

I can do this by a series of lines rigged from the after end of the tiller over blocks, and back into the saloon. By bracing my legs on the watertight door I can pull the tiller over to port or starboard. Hard work, but at least it gives my back a break. What makes it such hard work is that the lines have to be secured to the *after* end of the tiller. The reason for this is that I have only the jury tiller I rigged up after the proper tiller was broken in the storm.

Anyway, I lay down at 06.40 and I must have fallen asleep immediately. I awoke at 10.15 with the sails aback, having missed my schedule.

Now 106°F in the cockpit. I rigged an awning, but the flapping got on my nerves. I can stick the sun, no worse than the Middle East, and we used to go for *runs* in this, exercises with kit and gear. Few gave in. They were a hard lot, the Third Paras.

I'm eating a lot better now – I think it's with boredom rather than hunger. Any excuse to leave the tiller.

June 17th Contacted Portishead. What a joy, I really felt quite excited afterwards. Contacts all the way round, Portishead to Buenos Aires, to Falklands, to Wellington, to Sydney, to Perth, to Cape Town, and now back to Portishead. That's great news.

Spoke to Maureen, she sounded very sad and worried. I know that she's worried because we've no house, and it doesn't look like the one we were going to rent will be ready on time. I know she had her mind set on our own place after selling our own house. With the strain of this trip I'll be glad to get home so that I can take some of the worries and problems from her.

Filled a bucket with salt water, and sat at the tiller with my feet in the water. Very pleasant. I wish I could get the old drive back. I'm putting on weight, and I feel the difference. Actually I'm getting rather choked off – 18 hours on the tiller and no sleep is beginning to be a bit of a drag. With the sun beating down it's difficult to concentrate.

I'll stop whining. Not so far, and I'll be beating again into the NE Trades, and the Variables.

June 18th On the tiller all night. Tried a new system of sleeping and steering. Basically, I sleep beside the tiller, and every time she goes off course the sails bang, and I just reach across and put her back on course. I bundle my sleeping bag up as a support. It's not cold, and a pullover is enough to keep me warm. Then with my back resting on the sleeping bag and head on the pillow, which is on top of the teak round the cockpit, I rest my legs on the door frames. If she goes to port, the main backs, but is held by a preventer. If she goes to starboard the No 1 backs. In each case there is a noise and it wakes me.

I get about 20 minutes' sleep at a time, sometimes less. I've been on the tiller all day, and I don't feel tired after last night. So I'll give it a try again tonight.

June 19th Didn't spend the night on the tiller as planned. Got up to Force 6 (from ESE) so no need.

June 20th I put my sleeping bag under the tiller, and by raising the tiller I could lie under it. By lying on my right side I can see the instrument panel. If she goes off course

the sails slat and all I have to do is to look at the dials and
reach out and pull or push the tiller. I'm not so tired and
reckon I got about 4–5 hours of broken sleep.

I ought to tell you how I spend the day at the tiller, as
I'm fast becoming a zombie.

Dawn Crawled from beneath the tiller. Breakfast
Cornflakes, had to go to tiller twice to bring her back. On
deck hoisted ghoster, then on tiller.

10.00 Coffee – tiller.

13.15 Sight, worked it out in cockpit. Back and forth
from chart table to draw position line.

14.00 Lunch, two cups of coffee, tin mandarin oranges
eaten and drunk at the tiller.

16.00 Sight, worked out at the tiller. Back and forth
again.

18.30 I'm writing this by the tiller, and I've also had the
toilet, yes, and steered at the same time. Nothing over-
shadows the tiller.

I slept under the tiller again last night, even though
British Steel was sailing herself on the starboard tack on a
broad reach with a zephyr from the east. I stayed by the
tiller because every now and then a puff would come and she
would go close-hauled north east, and I'd have to pull her
round. The day's run worked out at 101 miles, which I
thought not bad, considering that there hadn't been much
wind. The barnacles were slowing her down. But it was no
good getting irritated about barnacles because there was
nothing I could do about them.

I'd been working on and off for weeks at remaking the
No 2 foresail, which had been blown out by a storm in the
Indian Ocean. It was a heavy task, requiring two panels to
be repaired with what seemed endless seams between them.
And each seam had to be stitched three times. Now I'd
nearly done the job. It really needed webbing to finish it off,

but I hadn't got any webbing, so I made do with rope, sewing it to the edges to help to take the strain. I was going to need that sail when we reached the NE Trades, and I didn't want to take any chances. If I didn't do it right, or strongly enough, it would blow out again as soon as I put it up. I couldn't bear the thought of that, so I worked and worked to make everything as strong as I could.

At 03.35 GMT on June 22nd we crossed the Equator, at 21° 38'W. This was the fourth time I'd crossed it, three times alone and once with Maureen. I didn't feel like celebrating and was more interested in finding a little red spider among the books on the chart table. I didn't kill it. What it lived on I have no idea, but I certainly had no wish to harm it.

Perhaps because of the spider, whose existence was a remarkable demonstration of *British Steel*'s ability to look after living creatures, I changed my mind about not celebrating the Equator. I decided to stand myself a haggis party.

CHAPTER NINE

Last Lap

It was a splendid feast, but I had to pay for it. I started with a cock-a-leekie soup, and washed down the haggis with about a quarter bottle of whisky. With perspiration pouring off me, I went through my repertoire of songs and poetry, starting with 'A man's a man for a' that' and finishing with the Hawick Festival Song. If there were any mermaids about at least they know more of Robbie Burns than they did before.

The payment came with a shocking head next morning. I'd not touched whisky for some weeks, and the quarter bottle which I consumed with such abandon exacted its tribute. But I felt it was worth it. I'd not been able to relax for what seemed ages, and I'm sure the evening did me good.

I woke early to a curious scratching sound, apparently coming from the hull. It was ever so faint, but it woke me – the slightest 'foreign' sound always does this, though you can sleep through a pandemonium of the familiar creaking blocks and screaming rigging. My first thoughts were that a shark might be scratching itself on the hull, then that it must be a flying fish floundering on deck. I looked round, but couldn't see anything. Still the noise went on, so I looked again, and eventually I found it; a stormy petrel which had managed to get itself caught under the mainsail, which was lying on deck. Poor little soul; it was shaking all over, and it ooked as if one of its wings was damaged. I took it below, and left it. When it had had time to recover a bit I examined t all over, and (although I'm no vet) it looked OK. So I took t outside and tossed it in the air. As soon as it was airborne, t flew off happily. Maybe it just didn't like sailing.

The wind was from the south, and *British Steel* sailed herself contentedly all day. What a joy it was to be able to eave the tiller! I re-read all the letters from home which I'd eceived at the rendezvous off Tasmania, and a chapter of *The Survival of Scotland*.

I had a scheduled contact with Portishead Radio on June 24th. The wind was still giving me an easy time and I was able to make telephone calls to Maureen, Phil Wolfinden and Frank Allen. Maureen still sounded very tense. I asked her to go away for a couple of weeks' rest, but she wouldn't. was worried by the amount of work she did, and felt ashamed of what seemed my own selfish voyage.

After my radio session, still enjoying freedom from the tiller, I lay down for half an hour. I could think only of the telephone calls, all concerned in one way or another with preparations for my arrival home. With time for reflection, I became more and more concerned – frightened would be a better word. I felt close to Bernard Moitessier, who gave up a good position in the *Sunday Times* £5,000 Round-the-World Race, and sailed off to Tahiti instead of going back to France. Was it all going to be lost, the feeling of well-being that the voyage gave me, of closeness to nature, of why we are really here? Now that the sailing was almost finished, would I lose my soul? I tried to pray, 'Please God, don't let me get wrapped up in avarice. Help me to salvage part of the way I now feel, to stay humble, honest, and with a feeling for others.'

I made that prayer as sincerely as I could, but I didn't want my feelings to turn to mere sentimentality so I got up to work. I finished the sewing of the No 2 foresail and I cleaned out the cooker. I felt, 'If I go down now, at least it can be said "He went with a clean cooker."'

I was now well past the northern limit of the South-east Trades, and fairly and squarely in the Doldrums. My log describes them:

June 25th Day's run 95 miles. Well, it's back to the tiller. Our wee holiday didn't last long, but it was a welcome break. What a lousy day's run ... Cirrus everywhere, and in every direction. Oh for those NE Trades, so as to get her close-hauled and put some miles in instead of these pathetic 100s. She hates these light winds – I think the Guinea Current may be against us. We're just on the edge.

June 26th Day's run 72 miles. What a bloody place. It's so frustrating. You see squalls coming, and you can wait until they hit, or change beforehand. But you've no idea as to the strength or direction of the squalls. I always wait. The squalls are so inconsistent. Ah well, can't last for ever.

June 27th Day's run 67 miles. It really doesn't seem worth the effort. I've been on duty now for just over 24 hours. Sails up and down, ghoster – No 1 – No 2 – No 1 – ghoster, and so on. The main track will be worn out shortly: the main is up and down like a yo-yo.

Big find – at long last I've found my blackcurrants and pears. Reason I couldn't find them before was that on top was a tin of celery soup. I always saw this tin, and never bothered to look any farther. Today two tins fell out, revealing the secret of the blackcurrants.

June 28th Circumnavigation complete. I've just recrossed my outward track, thereby completing my circumnavigation. My position for the recrossing was 7° 42'N, 26° 35'W. I really ought to be farther west. It's been pouring with rain for most of the day and I feel quite miserable. I have no feeling of achievement, relief or anything else. I just feel miserable. On my outward track the day I crossed (November 10th) the day's run was 163 miles noon to noon. So far I've covered 70 miles in about 24 hours.

I'm right in the middle of four shipping lanes and visibility is very low. I've my mizzen spreader light on, masthead and navigation lights when I'm below. I still doubt if they could see me. I only hope they are using their radar.

Got out the champagne and caviar, which I received from the British Ambassador in Cape Town. I'll toast everybody and everything tomorrow.

To try and snap out of my depression I had a wash and shave. As an antidote to depression it wasn't all that successful, for when I looked in the mirror I had a shock – I thought I looked about ninety. My eyes were black, and sunk deep into my head. I felt tired, both mentally and physically. But then I thought that there was a reasonable explanation for my tiredness: the storms of the Indian Ocean, followed by weeks of tiller-work without much sleep, were enough to account for it. I thought enviously of Robin Knox-Johnston's *Suhaili*, which would hold a course when running in light airs. But then I reflected that *Suhaili* would never go to windward like *British Steel*. Thrashing to windward was what *British Steel* was designed for. She had done her job damned well. Had I, I wondered, done mine anything like as well? Ought I to have been able to go faster? Did I make a tactical blunder by not getting farther south from New Zealand, and had I, perhaps, made another one by keeping too far east in the Atlantic now? I couldn't answer my own questions (I can't now). I *might* have gained by doing things differently at many different stages of the voyage; or I might have fared worse. What was done was done. It fell calm, so I turned in and prayed hard that I might find the North-east Trades soon. Then I went to sleep.

I got up at 07.30 for my link call to Portishead Radio. Phil Wolfinden wasn't at home, so I called Maureen and gave her details of my recrossing my outward track. She sounded cheerful, and much more her normal self. That cheered me immensely.

It was still raining – it had been raining steadily now for nearly 36 hours. There was a light wind from the south-east, about Force 2, and I sat at the tiller and kept her going at about 3 knots. Sitting in the warm rain and feeling that at least we were moving, I didn't feel so bad.

About 09.30 the wind backed to the north-east, and the rain stopped. I thought of my prayer last night – it seemed that it had been answered. The wind held all through the morning, and at lunchtime it was still blowing steadily. Feeling quite cheerful now, I went below and came back with one of the two bottles of champagne and the jar of caviar that the British Ambassador in South Africa had given to me. I had no champagne glass, so I used my pewter mug. I toasted everybody I could think of, and even gave Mr Neptune a wee drop. I had intended to eat only about one third of the caviar, but as the afternoon wore on, and the champagne was so very nice, somehow it all went.

Next day (June 30th) the wind still held from the northeast, or rather, from the north-north-east, and I felt fairly sure that we really had found the Trades. This was a happy day for me, but I was saddened by hearing on the radio of the death of the three Russian cosmonauts. It brought home the dangers that scientists still have to face. I felt deeply for their families.

Some big tunny fish appeared round *British Steel*. They were after the flying fish or so it seemed. These skimmed the water at terrific speeds, and suddenly a tunny would leap out of the water to intercept them in midair. I also saw a Portuguese man-o'-war of a most beautiful shade of pink. Normally, these jellyfish are blue, or a deep pink, but this one was a wonderful light pink.

Looking up from watching the fish, I saw, or thought I saw, a ship. At least, I saw the superstructure, and about half the hull. I went below for the binoculars, but when I got back on the deck the ship had disappeared. This worried me a good deal, for if a ship had been where I thought it was, it seemed too close to have disappeared so quickly. Of course, the visibility might suddenly have deteriorated round the ship so that it lost itself in a local haze – you can never be quite sure of this sort of thing at sea. But the visibility didn't look all that bad.

I didn't want to feel that I was starting to see things that weren't there, so I got out the chart of shipping routes for this part of the Atlantic. As far as I could estimate, the position of the ship I'd seen would have been right on the route from Rio de la Plata to Bishop's Rock. That eased my mind, for it suggested that there really had been a ship to see.

The routing chart indicated that I was in a triangle of shipping lanes – the Plate to England (Bishop's Rock), the West Indies to Freetown in Sierra Leone, and the Panama Canal to Cape Town. I decided to keep a watch that night.

July 1st brought me three telephone calls and a telegram, which I thought particularly nice, from John Malcolm at Port Chalmers in New Zealand. It said, 'Congratulations on achieving first solo anti-circumnavigation of the world.' It was a day of light winds interspersed with calms, but *British Steel* managed a day's run of 113 miles, which I thought pretty good. July 2nd brought me a decent wind, and we achieved 150 miles. Throughout the afternoon and evening I had a really wonderful sail. The wind was Force 3–4 from the north-east and *British Steel* was heeled over gently (about 15 degrees) and simply slicing through the water. I listened on the radio to the Ladies' Final at Wimbledon. I found it most exciting. Evonne Goolagong must be extraordinarily good. Hers was a fantastic achievement at nineteen.

Having feared that I was putting on weight, I was now concerned about losing it. For the past month I'd not felt much like eating – mainly, I think, because of the heat – and I now began to be afraid that when I got home my clothes would hang round me like a scarecrow. I didn't feel hungry, but I determined to force myself to eat more. I changed charts, and could now see England on my chart! That made me the more anxious to get myself looking fit.

My log records the little incidents of this penultimate stage of the voyage.

July 3rd Got up in the middle of the night to throw a fish back in. I could hear it flapping about all over the place. Just as I bent down to pick it up and throw it into the sea. I was hit on the head by another! I could only laugh. Mostly they have a sort of jelly round them, and the minute you touch them dozens of scales come off in your hands. I'll wash my hair tomorrow.

When dawn came I went on deck and tossed back 23 flying fish, mostly big ones. We must have gone through a big shoal of them.

Robin Knox-Johnston lost the NE Trades at 18° N, and he went as far as 41°W*. I doubt if I will get as far as 35°W this month, and I doubt if there is a lot to be gained by going far west. I think there will be a lot of calms with the Azores High. I'm banking on zephyrs, so that I can coast along at 2–3 knots, with the ghoster and mizzen staysail. I've also the light running sails. I hope I haven't made a serious blunder.

* RK-J was sailing back to England in April. I was sailing in July.

Opened second bottle of Drambuie last night. Very pleasant it was, too. Big prawn curry for dinner. I'm not having much success at putting weight on. I'll have to eat still more.

July 4th Day's run 168 miles. Haven't felt so hot, took a couple of Rennies. Bit of indigestion due to what I don't know.

Haven't looked at the tiller all day. We've been crashing along. I've the main up. It ought to be down when it gets up to Force 6, but I won't take it down. It's got to blow a lot harder than 6 before I drop it. I hope it doesn't blow out.

I could do a lot of work, but I'm not. I feel sure that we'll get a lot of calms in the Horse Latitudes, and this will give me something to do. I know how frustrated I get with calms.

(*Later*) I've been outside in the cockpit for about an hour, just leaning on the doghouse, watching the night pass. It really is something to sail a big yacht singlehanded, to see her heeled over and slicing her way through the water. I've had an enormous amount of pleasure from sailing *British Steel*. I must go each summer for a couple of days' sail singlehanded, just to reminisce and meditate.

The moon is out, the Plough is clear, and we're swinging along at 7–8 knots. Isn't this living? Just to be here is so exciting. I fear for the future. The trouble with this existence is that after a short period it's all gone, and you start dreaming again.

July 5th Got our position today, 20° 40′N, 32° 20′W. Day's run 168 miles. We've run 336 miles in two days, so I split it for the day's run, as I thought it would be about right.

Had a couple of nightcaps last night. The result was I slept in and missed my schedule with Portishead. Very

annoyed, as I'd arranged to talk to Maureen. Poor sou
she would have wasted the morning waiting for the cal
Tried to creep in at the end of a schedule that Portishea
had with another ship, but no good. He must have bee
using a different directional aerial from the one that pick
me up.

Luckily I did manage to tail in on a schedule wit
another ship. Portishead came through and said tha
they'd come back after they were finished with that cal
Would you believe it! A telegram from Maureen! All i
well, and I feel very contented. She couldn't take my ca
this morning anyway, as she was off to Scotland wit
Samantha. So I'm to call her on Friday (July 9th).

These technicians at Portishead really are tops. The
work really hard to get you through. If anyone thinks it
easy sitting working a set, they ought to try it. With inte
ference, and other ships, it takes patience and nursin,
The technician I always seem to get is Alan Huddart.
must own that I enjoy it when he comes up. Always chee
ful, and always with some snippet of news to tell m
Wimbledon or some other sport. I get embarrassed whe
I'm on the set. It seems that I cause no end of troubl
When I try to contact someone and he is not in, they wi
get another number from whoever answered the phon
they try that, and keep at it until they eventually get th
person. Considering that Portishead is probably th
busiest station in the world, it is one Government depar
ment nobody can fault.

July 6th 22° 5'N, 33° 10'W. Day's run 140 mile
Heard on the News about Louis Armstrong. What a los
Millions will mourn today. He was a great pioneer in jaz.
as well as a fantastic entertainer.

The NE Trades seem to be holding, but only just.
expect them to go soon.

Decided I must start organizing and getting cleaned u

What a thought! But I'm approx four weeks away, so I suppose I'll have to. Today I don't feel like rushing. I'm just enjoying the sail. I'll have to leave this feeling and have a concentrated effort to get through the Horse Latitudes.

July 7th 24° 23′N, 34° 25′W. Day's run 145 miles. It's now 11.00 (ship's time) and I still haven't started my work, contrary to what I said yesterday. I make excuses to myself about keeping myself occupied when it's calm. That's really all nonsense. There is *always* something to be done on board, so I could quite easily crash on and do some work. So why this passive feeling? I feel that my training and experience are warning me.

For a few nights now I've had a dream, actually more fantasy than dream. One dream was that men all covered in seaweed came on board, but when I shouted at them they went back into the sea. Another found me with my mother, Maureen and my sister Isabel all having a drink together. Other dreams are just as varied, and they don't seem to be linked.

Is something wrong to produce these feelings and thoughts? Could it be that I know I'll soon be in contact with people again, and it's having an effect? I remember the effect that people had on me off New Zealand and Tasmania. Could it be that the voyage is almost over, and I'm subconsciously digging my heels in so as to prolong the trip? But this doesn't seem right because of my attitude to get home within 300 days.

Or is it physical? Lack of vitamins? (I'm taking pills.) Or hunger? I'm not eating a great deal, but sufficient, I think. Salt has just occurred to me. I wonder? Again I don't think so, but I'll take some, anyway.

(*Later*) Have just met the ship *Throsdroft* (Norwegian) from Montreal bound for Cape Town. The ship came right across, and I didn't see her until she was almost up

on me. I didn't hear the diesel because she was downwind
but something made me go on deck. I was in the 'al
together', so down below, dressed (shorts) and then went
to hoist the signal Radio 2182. Damn me if the halyard
didn't blow out of my hand and go aloft! By that time she
was alongside. I hailed, 'Radio-Telephone'. Immediately
acknowledged, and on the set I spoke to the Captain (J.
Foshangen). He gave me my position. I had not long
taken a sight, and it was on the position line. So nothing
wrong in my sextant, or the navigation.

He made a U-turn and passed me again so that I could
take some photos. We then exchanged waves – the crew
were on deck, and they were all waving, too. He then
turned and headed south. I went back to the radio and we
had a yarn. He said that one of the crew suggested that I
should have a woman on board and not sail singlehanded!
People are always surprised when you say, 'singlehanded'.

The Captain said he'd report me to Lloyd's. He seemed
very pleasant and efficient. I told him about when I had
visited Norway with the Regiment. He asked about my
supplies, and I'm sure that had I asked he would have
lowered a boat and given me some. I really enjoyed that
meeting. Anyway, two things materialized. 1. I won't need
to worry about meeting people. 2. My navigation is spot
on.

July 8th 26°N, 35° 05′W. The NE Trades are holding,
and I'm delighted. My great fear was that we'd lose them
before this.

July 9th It looks as if the NE Trades are going now. I
can't complain.

July 10th Squally. It came from all directions all night,
but I stayed up and worked her and kept heading north. It
paid dividends. Noon sight put me 120 miles due north of
yesterday's sight. I was very pleased.

Still getting a load of dreams. I've increased my salt intake. Thirst? – urine shows no sign of dehydration. Hunger? I'm not eating a lot, so I'll increase, and see if that helps.

July 11th I've run out of water! I'm using my emergency, but I've plenty – three containers, and I'll catch some next squall.

July 12th Started work at last. I've cleaned out the stern and washed it. It will need more cleaning, but it's a lot better than it was. Eating a lot better, probably due to the work.

July 13th Last night I saw the most enormous swordfish. It really was very big indeed, I would have thought something like eight feet. Pity I hadn't the camera, but, of course, these situations are over so fast.

In a strange way the days now passed both quickly and slowly. Time went quickly because I had so much to do in getting *British Steel* spick and span for our homecoming, and I was getting more and more telephone calls as arrangements for our arrival began to be put in hand; but it also went slowly, because every patch of calm seemed doubly frustrating. For a brief period I had wondered if perhaps I could be home by the end of July, but that was scarcely possible. I might have managed the beginning of August, but that would not have suited anybody, because of Cowes Week. So I went back to my original estimate, made half the world away, of August 7th, with a private qualification, which later became public, that it might be a day or two earlier – as it duly turned out to be on August 6th.

On July 19th I celebrated Samantha's birthday with a party derived from the special pack of goodies that Maureen had prepared for the day. It contained a tin of chicken (whole), paté, potatoes, celery, apricots, ox tongue and tuna fish, and also a delicious cake made by Betty Ridley. What a party! That cake went a treat with sherry! July 21st brought the news that Maureen had settled in the house we had rented. She was always in my mind – poor soul she had had to sell and pack up our home when I left, and now she had to hunt for a house to rent, and move in. I marvelled at how she found the energy.

On July 23rd I met the first fishing boats of the return trip. They were tuna fishermen, small boats with great arm outriders, with all the lines trailing aft. One gave me quite a scare. I logged the incident:

The second one passed approx 100 yards across my bow. I put up an explosive, just in case no one was on deck, but there was. We were on a collision course, but as he had the right of way, I altered, almost gybing. There can be no doubt that if we had maintained first course we'd have collided, or at least I'd have gone through his lines. This would certainly have resulted in an insurance claim. I couldn't help wondering about his course. I wondered if he was having a bad season, and if a little claim on some old fishing lines would have helped matters.

Later I had second thoughts, and added:

I'm disgusted with myself over my thoughts about the tuna fishermen. Here am I, having spent ten months on my own, thinking and praying that if and when I return I would try to lead a better life. I feel humble and thankful for being so fortunate in life, yet I can still think these awful thoughts. Is it due to the number of telephone conversations that I'm slipping into our (human race) way of life and thoughts before I even step ashore? In our society we are always on our guard against being 'taken for a ride', or being 'conned'. I had thought that I'd left these thoughts long ago, but it seems not. Sad, very sad.

My next encounter with a ship restored my faith in the
Merchant Navy. A big ship came up from astern at night,
and I reckoned that he'd pass about a quarter of a mile
away, on my port beam. I wasn't carrying lights to save the
batteries, and I wasn't in danger, because it would have been
easy to move away from him. Just to be on the safe side,
when he was almost abeam, I flashed my torch on the sails
just once. Immediately he started searching for me with his
spotlight, and soon picked me up. Although I doubted if he
could see me in the cockpit, I waved. I know neither the
name nor the nationality of that ship, but whoever he was,
he was doing his job with real seamanship. If that officer of
the watch ever reads this, I should like him to know that I
was impressed by his behaviour. It is situations like that,
with a proper officer on watch, doing his job properly, which
wipe out the memory of those dreadful ocean ferrymen
whose biggest problem on watch seems to be what is going
to be in their sandwiches.

I was still having strange dreams. One began with my
going around the outside of *British Steel*, though whether I
was swimming or in a dinghy I don't know. Then, suddenly,
I was pacing up and down in a hotel room, and a man came
up to me. It was Bing Crosby, plain as a pikestaff. He asked
what the problem was, and I said I was doing the outside of
British Steel. He said 'This will help,' and he gave me a
polythene bag, adding, 'My father makes them.' Written
across the bag was 'Eric Hurst' (or perhaps 'Hurly'). I said,
'How will they help?' He said, 'You'll see,' and walked off.
That was all, or at least, I can't remember any more. It was
odd how these dreams persisted. I had never before experienced anything like them.

I listened on the radio to the broadcasts of the Apollo 15
expedition to the moon. I found them awe-inspiring, and felt
how little I had to show for my ten months alone at sea. I
also re-read the book on Donald Crowhurst, and found it

much more interesting than on the first reading.

So the days went by until a great moment on July 28th. I had a schedule with Portishead Radio and switched on the set to warm up. I was making some coffee while I waited when over the air came '*British Steel, British Steel*, this is *Ark Royal*'. I made a schedule with her, and when she came up I asked the operator if I could speak to the Captain, adding hastily, 'Or is it the Admiral?' A voice said, 'I'm the man who is in charge, and you've just promoted me to Admiral. I'm Captain John Roberts.'

I asked if he could pick me up on radar yet, and he said 'If you'll look astern, you'll see us.' Sure enough, there she was. What a sight! An aircraft carrier bearing towards you. I was thrilled.

A helicopter took off, and flew round me, taking photographs. As the *Ark Royal* passed, her decks were lined by her crew. By this time I'd got the ensign up, but not the burgee – unhappily there wasn't time for that.

As she passed abeam the crew gave three cheers and the band played. I was physically moved to have professional sailors showing such warmth to an amateur. I felt very humble. I dipped the ensign in salute, which was rather a tricky business, as it meant leaving the tiller.

Ark Royal circled a couple of times, and I was staggered to see her manoeuvrability. Captain Roberts handled her beautifully almost as if she were a yacht.

After she had gone, a remark of Captain Roberts' stayed in my mind. 'We ought to be thankful that it's a fine day,' he had said. That made me deeply conscious of the power which had been watching over me. I recalled that all my rendezvous had been in good conditions.

On July 31st an aeroplane chartered by the *Sunday Mirror* flew over me to take photographs. I knew that Maureen was on board, and just before the plane went off I thought I caught a glimpse of her. I waved frantically.

Early in the morning of Monday, August 2nd, HMS
Monkton (Lt-Commander R. Salt) found me. A boat from
the *Monkton* came across to ask if I wanted anything. I said
I didn't, but that a little water would come in handy as I
could do with an extra wash. They filled two jerry cans for
me.

Then HMS *Glasserton* (Lt-Commander Dean) arrived.
They didn't ask if I wanted anything, but sent across a bottle
of champagne, a chicken, a steak already seasoned, two
pints of milk and some potatoes! It really was very kind of
them, and I felt quite embarrassed by so much hospitality
and kindness. The *Glasserton* also sent across a walkie-
talkie set, so that I could be in communication without
having to work at my radio in the normal way.

I ought, I suppose, to have got on with my tasks of cleaning up, but the thought of the steak got the better of me, so I
had a steak-and-champagne lunch instead. I toasted the
officers and men of the *Glasserton*, of the *Monkton* and of
the whole Navy until the champagne was all gone. Then I
crawled into bed!

The Navy stayed with me, and made navigation very easy.
I was in touch with my escort via the walkie-talkie set, and
they simply told me what to do. They could see ships
coming on their radar, and told me exactly what action to
take.

At last came the reality of the moment I had dreamed
about for ten months – the end of the voyage. Frank Allen
on board *Blue Crystal*, had come out to lead me home to a
mooring at the Royal Southern Yacht Club.

CHAPTER TEN

An End – and a Beginning

I began this book by wondering where on earth to start; and now I don't know where to end. In truth, I don't think anything in life really has an end until life itself ends – and even then we don't know what comes next.

On Friday, August 6th, 1971, I walked on to the quay of the Royal Southern Yacht Club at Hamble 292 days after I'd left. The Prince of Wales, Princess Anne, the Duke of Edinburgh, the Prime Minister (Mr Edward Heath), a host of other notable people, and a great crowd of those who would call themselves ordinary people but who are the backbone of our country, were there to meet me. Mr Heath made a generous speech. With Maureen and Samantha by me I stood in front of a microphone and said what I could in reply.

People were wonderfully kind. *British Steel*, her sail down, rested safely at the quay. She looked as trim as I could make her, and people said nice things about the way she looked. The yacht, Robert Clark who designed her, and the men who built her deserved every word of praise that could be given. What could I feel, what can I feel, about myself?

Well, I did what I set out to do. I was incredibly lucky to be able to do what I wanted. I am conscious of how much I owe to others who helped me – nay, who made it possible or me – to achieve my voyage. Some (like Maureen) I have written about over and over again in this book. Others, the craftsmen who made components which stood up to everything the sea threw at them, those who wove the fabric for my sails, I do not even know. They were all my shipmates, although I sailed alone.

Was I selfish in demanding so much from Maureen, in leaving my wife and young daughter for the best part of a year while I undertook an adventure, in some ways a dangerous adventure, primarily because I wanted to? Yes, I think I must say that this was selfish. But having said that, I must go on to say that the answer to the question I ask myself is not really so simple. If life is to mean anything at all, a man must try to fulfil himself. For reasons I don't pretend to understand, because of the way I am made, I had to seek self-fulfilment in my voyage. Perhaps there must be an element of selfishness in any form of self-fulfilment. I think, at any rate, I hope, that the fulfilment is more important than the selfishness. It is Maureen's greatness that she understood this, that instead of trying to dissuade me, she accepted work, anxiety, separation, giving up our home – all the things that mean so much to every wife and mother – in order to help me to fulfil myself.

Was it worth it? I can answer this only by another question: who am I to say? For me, Chay Blyth, an individual human soul, the voyage was abundantly worth it. Ten months of solitude in some of the loneliest seas of the world strengthened every part of me, deepened every perception and gave me a new awareness of that power outside man which we call God. I am quite certain that without God's help many and many a time I could not have survived to complete my circumnavigation. I hope that I have brought home a new humility in my approach not only to other men, but to all living creatures. My logs reflect some of my thoughts and moods and feelings on these matters. Just how easy it is for good resolutions to evaporate is shown by my thoughts on my encounter with the tuna fishermen towards the end of the voyage. I checked myself then; I hope that I may be able similarly to check myself when angry or unworthy thoughts arise in the encounters of daily life. I say ' hope'. I can only say 'I hope'.

This, at least as far as I can put it into words, is what the voyage meant to me. Whether it meant anything to the rest of the world I do not know. I hope it did. That great concourse of people gathered at Hamble to see me come ashore brought a lump to my throat. I was deeply proud and flattered, and very, very grateful to them all; but I felt, and feel, that they were only partly there to see me, Chay Blyth. They were moved by something far beyond me personally, by the demonstration, of which I was merely the instrument, of *mankind*'s capacity to adventure and survive. To have been permitted to give such a demonstration is the justification of my voyage.

We need adventure. Mankind has always needed adventure, and perhaps we need it more than ever in the technological civilization of the twentieth century. I believe strongly in the value of adventure training such as the Outward Bound schools provide in helping young men and women to develop their whole personalities. If I can help to instil such feelings in others I shall feel that everything that went into my voyage, Maureen's part as well as mine, had purpose and meaning outside ourselves.

So I come not so much to the end of an adventure as to the beginning of a new chapter in our lives.

Stores

COMPILED BY MAUREEN BLYTH

My job was to look after the stores. The following list is not exhaustive. I have not attempted to include candles, scissors, radio spares, flags, fuses, and a million other small items. Neither have I listed the sailing equipment needed on the voyage.

MEDICAL

ANTISEPTIC

TCP	6 oz
Savlon antiseptic cream	
Vilan lanoline cream	1 tube
Germolene	2 tins

DRESSINGS

Sofra Tulle – dressing for burns	2 tins
Crepe bandages	2 × 3", 2 × 4"
Triangular bandage	
Elastoplast elastic adhesive plaster	
Adhesive plaster	2 × 3 yds × 1"
Adhesive bandages	2 × 5 yds × 3"
Absorbent gauze	6 yds
Elastoplast dressings	60
Airstrip dressings	2 tins
Cotton bandages	3 × 3", 3 × 2", 2 × 1"

Paraffin gauze	1 tin (36 pieces)
Zinc oxide strapping	1″ × 5 yds
Gypsona bandages	4
Cotton wool	1¼ lb
Lint	4 oz
Elastoplast airstrip wound dressings, waterproof	6

TABLETS

Dequadine lozenges	120
Oxytetracycline tablets – for infection	200
Celevac tablets	200
Vitamin B tablets	
Para-hypon tablets – for moderate pain	100
Thalazole tablets – for diarrhoea	500
Ducolax tablets – for constipation	200
Vitamin ACD tablets	400
Pethidine tablets 50 mg – for severe pain	50
Aluminium hydroxide tablets – for indigestion	100

NEEDLES, SYRINGES, SUTURES, BLADES

Ethicon sutures, No 2	2
Swan Morton blades, No 24	7
Swan Morton blades, No 11	6
Curved triangular – pointed needles for suturing, Nos 16 and 18	6
Sterile syringes	4
1½″ syringe needles	15
Omnipon ampoule syringes, ¼ gr morphine – for very severe pain	6
Xylocaine – local anaesthetic	40 ml

OTHER

Dental pack	
Toothache solution	10 ml
Antistine privine spray – nasal catarrh	1
Thermometers	2
Forceps	2

Optone eye drops – for eye infection   10 ml
Otosporin ear drops – for ear infection   5 ml
Cicatrin – antibiotic powder for wounds   15 G × 2
Tinaderm powder – for foot infections   100 G

FOOD

Irish Stew   2 doz
Steak & kidney   2 doz
Lamb & veg   2 doz
Beef & veg   2 doz
Spaghetti Bolognese   1 doz
Sweet corn   1 doz
Peas   2 doz
Carrots   2 doz
Celery soup   2 doz
Tomatoes   2 doz
Potatoes   2 doz
Mixed veg   2 doz
Steak & kidney pudding   2 doz
Corned beef   2 doz
Hams   6
Beef casserole   1 doz
Scotch Broth   1 doz
Vegetable salad   1 doz
Potato salad   1 doz
Tongues   2 doz
Braised mutton   1 doz
Steak & Kidney Pies   2 doz
Steak pasties   2 doz
Lamb Garni & Veg   1 doz
Braised steak   2 doz
Beans and minced beef   1 doz
Macaroni   1 doz
Raspberries   1 doz
Fruit salad   1 doz
Sultana   1 doz
Golden Honey Sponge Puddings   1 doz

Savoury minced steak	2 doz
Beans & pork sausage	1 doz
Oxtail soup	1 doz
Chicken soup	1 doz
Treacle Sponge Puddings	2 doz
Custard	2 doz
Plums	1 doz
Celery	2 doz
Mushroom soup	2 doz
Blackcurrants	1 doz
Pears	1 doz
Mandarin oranges	1 doz
Peaches	1 doz
Strawberries	1 doz
Condensed milk	2 doz
Evaporated milk	2 doz
Nestlé's cream	2 doz
Sardines	2 doz
Royal Game Soup	1 doz
Prawns	1 doz
Salmon	1 doz
Tuna	1 doz
Walls pork sausages	1 doz
Butter	7
Luncheon meat	6
Mushrooms	9
Kippers	2 doz
Haggis	1 doz
Tomato ketchup	1 doz
Sandwich spread	1 doz
Ideal Sauce	1 doz

DEHYDRATED FOOD

Chow Mein	24 pkts
Chicken Bombay with rice	1 doz
Beef Casserole & Dumplings	1 doz
Savoury Beef and Potato Nests	1 doz

pkts each containing
Garden peas dried   12 lb
Smash   3
Smashers   3
pkts each containing
Dried Mixed Veg   1 lb
Smashers   3
Smash   3
Dried onion tubs   2
Mixed green/red peppers   2
pkts each containing
Smash   3
Smashers   3
Mixed veg tubs   4
Pepper tubs   2
Onions   2
ong-life milk   150 pints
ggs   30 doz
elloggs Variety Packs   1 doz
orridge oats   2 pkts
cobs Cream Crackers   2 doz
yvita   1 doz
uc biscuits   1 doz
arge Oxo   1 doz

RINK
hisky   6
in   6
rambuie   6
uinness   20 doz

AVIGATION BOOKS

ntarctic Pilot
ew Zealand Pilot
ustralian Pilot
frica Pilot Vol I
frica Pilot Vol II

South America Pilot Vol I
South America Pilot Vol II
Nautical Almanac 1970 and 1971
List of Lights A, D, G, K

Tables of Computed Altitude & Azimuth
  0° – 14° Vol I
15° – 29° Vol II
30° – 44° Vol III
45° – 59° Vol IV

BBC World Service Programmes
and Recommended Frequencies
Charts Applicable to Voyage

RADIO

Marconi Kestrel Mark III (radio telephone)
610 Clifford and Snell Lifeline Radio (emergency set)
Zenith Oceanic Portable (for time signals, news and pleasure)
Brookes and Gatehouse Homer/Heron Direction Finding
  Equipment and Converter for time signals

CLOTHING

Shirts	1 doz
Sports shirts	1 doz
Pullovers	7
Trousers	4 pairs
Socks	2 doz
Underclothes	2 doz
Handkerchiefs	1 doz
Towels	1 doz
Pyjamas	3 pairs
Gloves	2 pairs
Wellingtons	4 pairs
Sailing shoes	2 pairs
Diving suit	1

iling boots	4 pairs
orts	2 pairs
nglasses	2 pairs
oppy hat	1
iling suits	3

DDING

eping bags	2
ctic sleeping bag	1
ace blankets	3
eping-bag liners	3
lowcases	6

JRVIVAL PACK (Permanently ready)

× Solar still, torch, batteries, shark repellent,
iograph, space blanket, matches, knife, small
mpass, robe, first-aid kit, fishing equipment,
oculars, explosives.
od-pack A (emergency food)
allons water
ares

THE LUNATIC EXPRESS

Charles Miller

The magnificent saga of how the white man changed Africa — the pioneers, visionaries and politicians — and their crazy railway.

"All in all a great adventure, a great slice of the human comedy bound up in a huge book with something for everybody."
—*Boston Sunday Herald Traveler*

With 32 pages of photos

$1.95

HORATIO HORNBLOWER

C. Northcote Parkinson

♦

From papers discovered just recently, C. Northcote Parkinson, presents a complete, full-length biography of this great naval hero, a seaman second only to Nelson in the annals of British naval history.

"There is enough here to delight even the most enthusiastic of Hornblower's fans."
                                        —LOS ANGELES TIMES

With 32 pages of photographs

$1.50